QUICK AND EASY CROCHET PROJECTS WITH  YARN

AMIGURUMI PLUSHIES

METEOOR BOOKS

Amigurumi Plushies
Quick and Easy Crochet Projects with Chunky Yarn
Theresa's Crochet Shop

Copyright © 2024 Meteoor BV (BE0550756201)

 Have you made creations with patterns from this book?
Share your creations on *www.amigurumi.com/5200*
or on Instagram with *#amigurumiplushies*

First published November 2024
by Meteoor BV, Antwerp, Belgium
www.meteoorbooks.com
hello@meteoorbooks.com

Text and images © 2024 Theresa's Crochet Shop
Printed and bound by Grafistar

ISBN 978-949164-354-5

D/2024/13.531/4

A catalogue record for this book is available from the Royal Library
of Belgium.

QUICK AND EASY CROCHET PROJECTS WITH **CHUNKY** YARN

AMIGURUMI
PLUSHIES

This book is dedicated to…

MY GRANDMA, WHO TAUGHT ME HOW IMPORTANT IT IS TO BE SILLY!

If you're reading this book, you either already love crocheting with plush yarn or (I have a feeling) you are about to!

After years of making amigurumi with acrylic yarn, I decided to try crocheting a plush animal. I wasn't sure if I would like the result; I certainly didn't expect to LOVE it! There's something magical about making animals bigger, softer, and more snuggly just by choosing plush yarn. The soft yarn sets the perfect depth and texture to bring these little animals to life with sparkly eyes, pink cheeks, and big floppy ears or itty-bitty arms. If you're like me, when you finish crocheting each plushie, you'll see their unique personality shining through and will want to name them and even grab them their favorite snack! :)

Whether you are a beginner or an experienced "amigurumist," I hope that making these animals will bring you as much joy as it has brought me over the years. I discovered amigurumi in 2011, and it has been such a gift to me. Creating little animals to give away or sell kept me busy during the long years that I waited and hoped to become a mom, and it is now the perfect way to relax after my boys are in bed.

I am incredibly grateful for the opportunity to design the snuggly animal friends for this book. My #1 goal is always to keep my patterns easy to follow, so they can provide you with a relaxing break after a long day or make the perfect custom gift.

Thank you, thank you for choosing my book! Now it's time to cuddle up with your hook and yarn and create your own amigurumi plushies!

Theresa

LET ME INTRODUCE YOU TO AMIGURUMI!

These adorable toys are crocheted in a style that originated in Japan. The word *"amigurumi"* combines *"ami"* (meaning *"crocheted"* or *"knitted"*) and *"nuigurumi"* (meaning *"stuffed toy"*). When you create amigurumi, you crochet in a continuous spiral without joining rounds or turning your work, which results in cute, three-dimensional shapes that you can sew together to make your toy.

EVERYTHING YOU NEED

Yarn

I made the amigurumi in this book with plush *chenille* yarn. This type of yarn also goes by the name of *velvet* or *blanket* yarn. Plush yarn is super soft to the touch, but challenging to work with. I'll explain all about this yarn and give some advice on how to crochet with it comfortably on page 9.

Don't feel tied to my yarn choices——any weight of cotton, acrylic, or wool will work. If you do change the yarn weight, just make sure to adjust your hook size accordingly. Check out the chart below for a quick comparison of yarn weights and the recommended hook sizes. One important tip: when crocheting amigurumi, use a slightly smaller hook than what's recommended on the yarn label. This way, your stitches will be tighter, and the stuffing won't show through.

The yarn quantities listed in the patterns are estimates. They may vary depending on how tightly or loosely you crochet. You can use leftover yarn from other projects or start with a new ball.

Crochet Hook

Crochet hooks come in various sizes and materials. Bigger hooks make bigger stitches, while smaller hooks create finer stitches. It's crucial to match the right hook size with the right yarn weight. For amigurumi in plush yarn, you'll generally want to use a hook two or three sizes smaller than recommended on the yarn label. However, if you crochet tightly, you might want to consider using a slightly larger hook to prevent the plush

I work with these weights

NUMBER (SYMBOL)	2	3	4	5	6	7
CATEGORY NAME	fine	light	medium	heavy	very heavy	super heavy
UK YARN TYPE	4 ply	double knitting (DK)	aran	chunky	super chunky	jumbo
US YARN TYPE	sport	light worsted	worsted	bulky	extra bulky	ultra / roving
THE HOOK I RECOMMEND IN US SIZE	B-1	B-1 to E-4	E-4 to 7	7 to I-9	H/8 to M/13	L/11 and larger
THE HOOK I RECOMMEND IN METRIC SIZE	2.5mm	2.5 to 3.5mm	3.5 to 4.5mm	4 to 5.5mm	5 to 9mm	8 to 10mm

yarn from snapping under too much pressure. I recommend using a plastic or metal hook, as they tend to slip through stitches more easily. If possible, choose a hook with a rubber ergonomic handle for added comfort. My absolute favorite hook when working with plush yarn is the *Prym Ergonomic Crochet Hook.*

Stitch Marker

A stitch marker is a simple yet essential tool. It's a small metal or plastic clip that helps you keep track of your starting point and ensures you've made the correct number of stitches in each round. Mark the last stitch of your round with the stitch marker, then move it up one round at the end of each round. When you reach the stitch marker after completing a new round, take it out, crochet that stitch, and then place the marker in the last stitch you crocheted.

Stuffing

For filling your amigurumi, I recommend polyester fiberfill. It's washable and non-allergenic. As you crochet, stuff the individual parts of your toy. Begin stuffing wider pieces like the head or body when they are about halfway finished. For very thin pieces where you can't fit in a finger, use the back of a crochet hook or a chopstick. Remember, it's important to use more stuffing than you might initially think. If the toy isn't stuffed tightly enough, it will lose its shape over time. However, avoid overstuffing, as it can stretch the fabric and make the stuffing visible. Finding the right balance is key.

Note: Because plush amigurumi are much larger, they require a greater amount of stuffing. Without enough stuffing, the finished amigurumi may look floppy or flat in some areas, and might also appear lumpy.

Safety Eyes

For these designs, I use safety eyes. These come in two parts: the front bead with a ribbed stem and the back washer. The washer keeps the eye securely in place. Be cautious

when applying safety eyes—once the washer is on, you can't remove it, so make sure the post is exactly where you want it before attaching the washer. If you're making toys for children under three, it's safer to embroider the facial features instead.

Note: I've used Trapezoid-shaped safety eyes, some of which I have painted by hand. To do so, I take a clear, plastic safety eye, and paint it on the inside with glittery nail polish or acrylic paint. I apply 2-3 thin coats for maximum glitter.

Tapestry Needle

For embroidery, you'll need a long tapestry needle with a rounded tip. The rounded tip makes it easier to insert your needle into specific spaces without splitting the yarn. A bent-tip tapestry needle helps even more with ease of sewing.

Sewing Pins

Sewing pins are handy to have around. They help you position the body parts before sewing them on permanently, so you can double-check the placement from all angles.

PLUSH YARN, AND HOW TO WORK WITH IT

Plush yarn is a popular choice for creating soft, cozy items. This yarn is available in various thicknesses, typically ranging from bulky (5) to jumbo (7). Here's what you need to know about working with plush yarn.

What is it made of?

All plush yarn is technically *chenille* yarn (but it also goes by the commercial names of *velvet* or *blanket* yarn). It's not hard to see the resemblance of this fiber's namesake, as *'chenille'* is the French word for caterpillar. Chenille yarn is made by taking short lengths of yarn between two core threads, twisting them together and then cutting them to achieve a pile effect. These yarn edges stand at right angles to the yarn core, resulting in a super soft, sleek fabric. To prevent patches of the pile from coming apart, low-melt nylon is added to the yarn core. Afterward, the yarn is steamed to make sure the pile stays put.

This yarn not only looks like, but also feels like a fuzzy caterpillar. It is made entirely of polyester, a synthetic fiber which is a type of plastic, making it durable and soft, but sensitive to heat. High temperatures can melt the fibers, so avoid ironing and check the label for care instructions, as some chenille yarns are not machine washable.

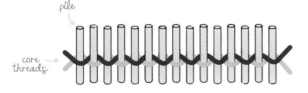

Advantages of Using Plush Yarn

Plush yarn is ideal for creating huggable toys. It transforms small amigurumi projects into larger, snuggly items that children will love. Some benefits of using plush yarn include:

- **Faster Work-Up:** It's much thicker than regular cotton or acrylic yarn and can transform the same mini amigurumi into a huggable plushie! Because of the thickness of the yarn, the stitches are larger, making these amigurumi pieces work up a lot faster.
- **Fluffier Finish:** The final toy is softer, with fewer visible gaps in the stitches.

Tips for Working with Plush Yarn

If you are just starting out and figuring out how to crochet amigurumi, then plush yarn might not be the easiest place to start. Although it works up super quickly, and the end result is super snuggly and soft, there is a bit of a learning curve. Here are some tips to help you work with this material:

- **Seeing Stitches:** Initially, you might find it hard to see the stitches. Don't be surprised if you find yourself unsure of where to start or end. Be patient and go slowly. Use your fingers to feel the stitches. With practice, you'll be able to see the stitches more clearly.
- **Gentle Handling:** Plush yarn is fragile and breaks easily when sewing. Avoid tight tension and be gentle.
- **Unraveling:** If you need to unravel your work after you've made a mistake, do so slowly and carefully to avoid shedding and tangling. It might be easier to "correct" your mistake in a next round by making an extra increase or decrease.
- **Magic Ring:** When making a magic ring, start with loose tension to avoid breaking the yarn when pulling it closed. Gently wiggle the yarn tail to close the center slowly. You can find a few alternatives to the magic ring technique on page 18 (starting a circular piece with 2 ch stitches, starting

a circular piece with an open ring).

- **Sewing Pieces Together:** Sewing with plush yarn can be tricky. The friction caused by threading it into the eye of a needle as well as the weaving in and out of the stitches causes shedding. Consider using a regular acrylic or cotton yarn in a matching color for attaching larger pieces. When sewing with plush yarn, use a large sewing needle and sew slowly and gently to prevent the yarn from breaking.
- **Shedding:** Shedding is common with chenille yarn. After you cut a piece of yarn, you will get free flowing shedding flakes coming out from the yarn ends. You can tie a knot at the end, using the two thin core threads.
- **Color Choice:** If you're a beginner, avoid using dark colors, as the stitches are harder to see. Lighter, colorful yarns are easier to work with.
- **Yarn Quality:** Use high-quality plush yarn to minimize issues with fraying and breaking. I advise some brands I like to work with below.

→ Although plush yarn can be challenging, especially for beginners, the results are worth the effort. The finished products are **soft, fluffy, and perfect for cuddling**. With patience and practice, you'll find working with plush yarn becomes easier and more enjoyable.

Note: *Once the toy is crocheted, the risk of the yarn breaking is minimal. The stitches form a firm fabric, making the toy durable and ready for playful handling.*

Yarn Brands

Here are some commonly available yarn brands which I've become familiar with:

- **Parfait Chunky (6) by Premier Yarns:** Super soft and one of the best plush yarns I've used, with minimal shedding, my favorite.
- **Parfait Chunky XL (7) by Premier Yarns:** A jumbo version of Parfait Chunky. It's very soft but sheds easily when sewing, so consider using acrylic yarn for joining pieces.
- **Honey Bunny (6) by Hobbii:** Equally soft with average shedding; recommended.
- **Baby Snuggle (6) by Hobbii:** Similar to Honey Bunny but offers different color options.
- **Toucan (6) by Hobbii:** Less soft but sheds a bit less.
- **Estako Velvet (6):** Comparable with Parfait Chunky and Honey Bunny, with average shedding.
- **Sweet Snuggles Lite (6) by Loops and Threads:** Soft but limited in color options. It's thicker than other (6) plush yarns, making it unsuitable for mixing with them.
- **Sweet Snuggles (7) and Chenille Home Yarn (7) by Loops and Threads:** Lovely jumbo weight yarns with average shedding. Good for seeing stitch definition, ideal for beginners.
- **Flutterby Chunky (5) by James C Brett:** A thinner yarn that is soft with average shedding.
- **Chenille (5) by Paintbox Yarns:** My skein shed excessively, making it hard to work with.

Some other brands which I haven't tried, but they have decent reviews:

- **Plush by Big Twist (from JOANN)**
- **Bambi by Katia**
- **Dolphin Baby by Himalaya Yarn**
- **Velvet by Himalaya Yarn**
- **Yummy by King Cole**
- **Velvet by DMC**
- **Luxury velvet by Schachenmayr**
- **Velvet by Bernat**

Blanket yarn is not as soft as the plush brands mentioned above but doesn't shed or snap, making it a popular alternative. It is usually labeled as weight 6 but works up thicker than plush #6 yarns:

- **Premier Basix Chenille Brights (6) by Premier Yarns**
- **Velluto (6) by Alize** (from yarnstreet.com)
- **Cozy Occasion by Yarn Bee** (from Hobby Lobby)
- **Blanket Yarn by Bernat**

Yarn alternative:

- **Feels Like Butta Thick & Quick by Lion Brand:** Similar feel to chenille yarn but due to its different and more sturdy chainette construction, it has less fuzz.

Frustrated about working with plush yarn?

All toys in this book can be made with regular cotton yarn as well. While working with plush yarn, you will end up with a big huggable toy; when crocheting these designs with regular cotton or acrylic yarn, you'll have a palm-sized toy to play.

Note: When working with a different yarn weight, you'll want to change the size of the safety eyes to match your animal's head size.

→ *Important: When using cotton or acrylic yarn, the body and/or head of your animal might appear a bit too short. Plush yarn tends to visually elongate the body, so to compensate, you will want to add 1 to 3 extra rounds of single crochet to the body.*

made with cotton yarn

made with chenille yarn

WHAT TO KNOW BEFORE YOU START

Pattern Structure

These patterns are worked in continuous spirals. Crocheting in spirals can be confusing since there's no clear indication of where a new round begins and the previous one ends. To keep track of the rounds, you can mark the end of a round with a stitch marker or safety pin. After crocheting the next round, you should end up right above your stitch marker. Move your stitch marker at the end of each round to keep track of where you are.

At the beginning of each line you will find 'Rnd + a number' to indicate which round you are in. If a round is repeated, you'll read 'Rnd 9 – 12', for example. You then repeat this round four times, crocheting the stitches in round 9, 10, 11 and 12.

Although we usually crochet in rounds, occasionally it happens that we switch to rows, going back and forth instead of working in continuous spirals. When we switch to rows, it will be indicated with 'Row + a number'. You end the row with a ch 1 and turn your crochetwork to start the next. Don't count this turning chain as a stitch and skip it when working the next row (unless otherwise mentioned).

At the end of each line you will find the number of stitches you should have in square brackets, for example [9]. When in doubt, take a moment to check your stitch count.

When parts of the instructions repeat throughout the round, we place them between rounded brackets, followed by the number of times this part should be worked. We do this to shorten the pattern and make it less cluttered.

Counting Stitches

Counting stitches will help ensure that you are following the pattern correctly. When counting stitches, you do not count the slip knot or the loop on the hook (this is the working loop). The easiest way to count stitches is to look at the plaited tops (V's at the top of your crochetwork). If you discover you missed a stitch or made one too many, you can try to correct it by making an (extra) increase or decrease in the following round.

Counting Chain Stitches

Each V-shaped chain counts as one stitch. Never count your first slip knot and the loop on the hook. Make sure that the chain is untwisted and the front is directed towards you for easier counting.

Amigurumi Gallery

With each pattern, we have included a URL and QR code that will take you to that character's dedicated online gallery. Share your finished amigurumi, find inspiration in the color and yarn choices of your fellow crocheters and enjoy the fun of crocheting. Simply follow the link or scan the QR code with your mobile phone. Phones with iOS will scan the QR code automatically in camera mode. For phones with Android you may need to activate QR code scanning or install a separate QR Reader app.

**Counting stitches in plush yarn can be quite challenging.
Here are some tips to make it easier:**

1. **Use good lighting:** Adequate lighting helps you see the stitches more clearly, making it easier to count them accurately.
2. **Feel out the stitches:** Sometimes the "core" of the yarn can be easily felt by touch. Try to feel your stitches instead of relying solely on sight. Pinching around the stitches can help you identify them. After completing a few rounds, you should be able to get a feel for where your stitches are as you learn the new yarn and hook tension.
3. **Count and divide:** Divide your round into sections. Use extra stitch markers if it helps, and know how many stitches need to be in each section. This way, you can keep track of your progress in smaller steps.
4. **Don't stress over minor mistakes:** Don't be overly concerned if you have an extra stitch or are one stitch short. Unless you're off by 3 or 4 stitches or more, it usually won't make a big difference in the final product, and you can correct it in the next round.

STITCHES

If this is your first time making amigurumi, you might find it useful to have a tutorial at hand. With the stitches explained on the following pages, you can make all of the amigurumi in this book. I suggest you practice the basic stitches before you start making one of the designs. This will help you to read the patterns and abbreviations more comfortably, without having to browse back to these pages.

This book is written in US crochet terms.

STITCH TUTORIAL VIDEOS

With each stitch explanation I have included a URL and QR code that will take you to an online stitch tutorial video (left-handed tutorials available through the same link), showing the technique step by step to help you master it even more quickly. Simply follow the link or scan the QR code with your smartphone. Phones with iOS will scan the QR code automatically in camera mode. For phones with Android you may need to install a QR Reader app first.

HOLD THE HOOK & YARN (HAND POSITION)

Usually, we handle the hook with the same hand we use to write, but it's not a rule. If you take it with your right hand, you will crochet from right to left. If you take it with your left hand, you will crochet from left to right. There are different ways of holding a crochet hook. You will need to experiment and find the way that feels the most comfortable for you.

Pencil grip
Hold the hook as you would a pencil, grasping it between your thumb and index finger, in the middle of the flat thumb rest. Your middle finger is positioned on the other side to balance the hook.

Knife grip
Hold the hook in the same manner as you would hold a knife, grasping it between your thumb on one side and index and middle finger on the other side, resting the end of the hook against your palm.

Hold the yarn
The free hand holds your crochet work and at the same time controls the tension of the yarn. You can weave the yarn through your fingers or just place the thread between your palm and two or three fingers. Keep in mind that you have to maintain a steady tension while crocheting, so that your stitches come out even.

Tension
It can be challenging to master the tension of your yarn when you are new to crochet. You are not alone — tension is the one thing that most beginning crocheters have a hard time with. To maintain tension in the working yarn, you may find it helpful to unravel a long end of your yarn ball (your tension is tighter when the weight of the ball pulls your yarn tight), and wrap the yarn around the fingers of the hand opposite the one holding the hook.

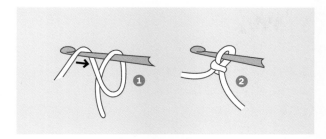

SLIP KNOT

Tying a slip knot onto the crochet hook is one of the first things you need to know to get started with crocheting. It's like casting the yarn onto the hook so you can start crocheting.

Step 1: Wrap the yarn into a loop, so that the shorter strand lies behind the longer one. Insert the crochet hook through the loop, catch the longer yarn and bring it through the loop.

Step 2: Pull on both ends of the yarn to tighten the knot around the hook.

Scan or visit **www.stitch.show/ slipknot** for the video tutorial

YARN OVER HOOK

The yarn over hook technique is used in every type of crochet stitch. Wrap the yarn over the hook from back to front. The yarn is now wrapped around the tip of the crochet hook, so that the hook can grab and pull the yarn.

Scan or visit **www.stitch.show/yoh** for the video tutorial

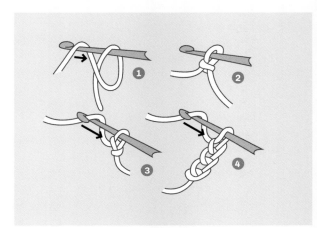

CHAIN [abbreviation: ch]

If you're working in rows, your first row will be a series of chain stitches.

Step 1: Use the hook to draw the yarn through the loop.

Step 2: Pull the loop until tight.

Step 3: Wrap the yarn over the hook from back to front. Pull the hook, carrying the yarn, through the loop already on your hook. You have now completed one chain stitch.

Step 4: Repeat these steps as indicated in the pattern to create a foundation chain.

Scan or visit **www.stitch.show/ch** for the video tutorial

INSERT THE HOOK (PLACEMENT OF STITCHES)

With the exception of chains, all crochet stitches require the hook to be inserted in existing stitches. Insert the hook underneath both top loops of the stitch in the row or round below. When inserting the hook, you take it from front to back through a stitch. The point of the hook must always look down or sideways, so the hook doesn't snag the yarn or the fabric.

When asked to crochet FLO or BLO you make the same stitch but leave one loop untouched.

Inserting the hook in front loops only (abbreviation: FLO)
When working in Front Loops Only, you pick up only the front loop towards you.

Inserting the hook in back loops only (abbreviation: BLO)
When working in Back Loops Only, you pick up only the back loop away from you.

Scan or visit **www.stitch.show/FLO-BLO** for the video tutorial

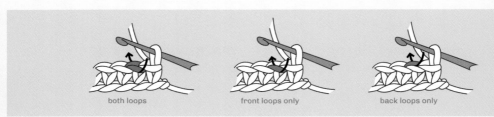

both loops   front loops only   back loops only

SINGLE CROCHET (abbreviation: sc)

Single crochet is the stitch that will be most frequently used in this book.

Step 1: Insert the hook into the next stitch

Step 2: Wrap the yarn over the hook. Pull the yarn through the stitch. You will see that there are now two loops on the hook.

Step 3: Wrap the yarn over the hook again and draw it through both loops at once.

Step 4: You have now completed one single crochet.

Step 5: Insert the hook into the next stitch to continue.

Scan or visit **www.stitch.show/sc** for the video tutorial

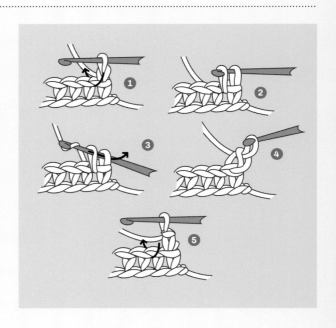

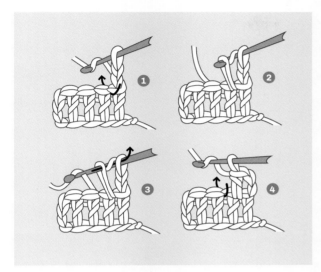

HALF DOUBLE CROCHET

(abbreviation: hdc)

Step 1: Bring your yarn over the hook from back to front before placing the hook in the stitch.

Step 2: Wrap the yarn over the hook and draw the yarn through the stitch. You now have three loops on the hook.

Step 3: Wrap the yarn over the hook again and pull it through all three loops on the hook. You have completed your first half double crochet.

Step 4: To continue, bring your yarn over the hook and insert it in the next stitch.

Scan or visit
www.stitch.show/hdc
for the video tutorial

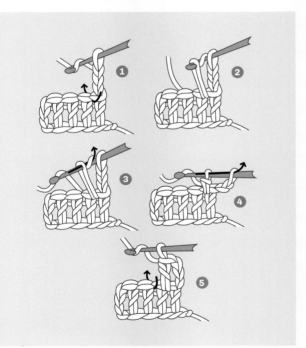

DOUBLE CROCHET (abbreviation: dc)

Step 1: Bring your yarn over the hook from back to front before placing the hook in the stitch.

Step 2: Wrap the yarn over the hook and draw the yarn through the stitch. You now have three loops on the hook.

Step 3: Wrap the yarn over the hook again and pull it through the first two loops on the hook. You now have two loops on the hook.

Step 4: Wrap the yarn over the hook one last time and draw it through both loops on the hook. You have now completed one double crochet.

Step 5: To continue, bring your yarn over the hook and insert it in the next stitch.

Scan or visit
www.stitch.show/dc
for the video tutorial

Scan or visit
**www.stitch.show/
slst** for the video
tutorial

SLIP STITCH (abbreviation: slst)

A slip stitch is used to move across one or more stitches at once or to finish a piece.

Step 1: Insert your hook into the next stitch.

Step 2: Wrap the yarn over the hook and draw through the stitch and loop on your hook at once.

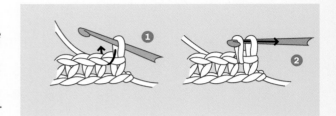

INVISIBLE DECREASE (abbreviation: dec)

When decreasing, two stitches are crocheted together. The number of stitches in a round therefore decreases and the piece shrinks.

Step 1: Insert the hook in the front loop of your first stitch. Now immediately insert your hook in the front loop of the second stitch. You now have three loops on your hook.

Step 2: Wrap the yarn over the hook and pull it through the first two loops on the hook.

Step 3: Wrap the yarn over the hook again and pull it through the remaining two loops on the hook. You have now completed one invisible decrease.

Scan or visit
www.stitch.show/dec
for the video tutorial

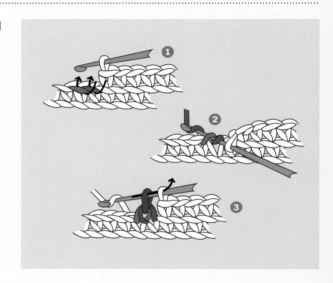

Scan or visit
www.stitch.show/inc
for the video tutorial

INCREASE (abbreviation: inc)

To increase, two single crochet stitches are made in the same stitch. This way, new stitches are created and the piece expands.

Step 1: Make a first single crochet stitch in the next stitch.

Step 2: Make a second single crochet stitch in the same stitch.

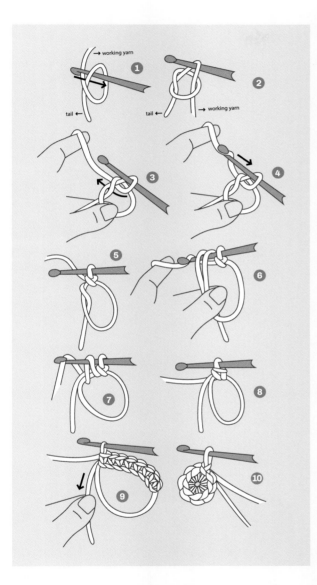

MAGIC RING

To start an amigurumi piece, you need a little circle. A magic ring is the ideal way to start crocheting in the round as there will be no hole left in the middle of your starting round. You start by crocheting over an adjustable loop and finally pull the loop tight when you have finished the required number of stitches.

Step 1: Start with the yarn crossed to form a circle.

Step 2: Draw up a loop with your hook, but don't pull it tight.

Step 3: Hold the circle with your index finger and thumb and wrap the working yarn over your middle finger.

Step 4-5: Make one chain stitch by wrapping the yarn over the hook and pulling it through the loop on the hook.

Step 6: Now insert your hook into the circle and underneath the tail. Wrap the yarn over the hook and draw up a loop.

Step 7: Keep your hook above the circle and wrap the yarn over the hook again.

Step 8: Pull it through both loops on the hook. You have now completed your first single crochet stitch. Continue to crochet **(repeating step 6, 7, 8)** until you have the required number of stitches as mentioned in the pattern.

Step 9-10: Now grab the yarn tail and pull to draw the center of the ring tightly.

You can now begin your second round by crocheting into the first single crochet stitch of the magic ring. You can use a stitch marker to remember where you started.

Scan or visit
**www.stitch.show/
magicring** for the
video tutorial

TIP: Making a magic ring with plush yarn can be quite challenging, as the yarn may snap when too much force is applied. To avoid this, **crochet your stitches loosely** and **gradually tighten the magic ring** as you complete each stitch.

If this method doesn't work for you, there are two alternative techniques you can try: starting a circular piece with two chain stitches (page 18) or beginning with an open ring (page 18).

STARTING A CIRCULAR PIECE WITH TWO CHAIN STITCHES

Scan or visit
www.stitch.show/2ch
for the video tutorial

Step 1: Start by making a slip knot. Then, make 2 chain stitches and work x sc into the second chain from the hook—where x is the number of sc stitches you would make in your magic ring.

Step 2: You now have a little circle to start with. Start your next round in the first sc stitch.

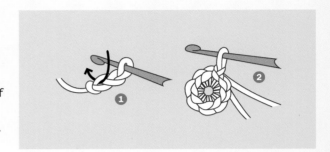

STARTING A CIRCULAR PIECE WITH AN OPEN RING

Scan or visit
www.stitch. show/ring for the video tutorial

Step 1: start with 6 chain stitches and close with a slip stitch in the first chain to make a ring.

Step 2: Insert your hook into the center of the ring, instead of into the chain stitch and complete the stitch in the usual way. Follow the pattern instructions to determine how many stitches to work into the ring.

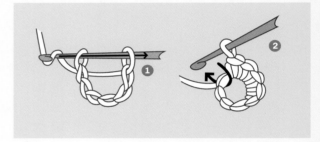

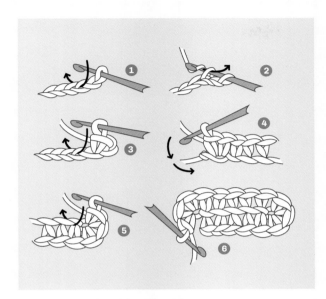

WORKING AROUND A FOUNDATION CHAIN

Some pieces start with an oval. You make an oval by crocheting around a foundation chain.

Step 1: Crochet a foundation chain with as many chains as mentioned in the pattern and skip the first chain on the hook.

Step 2-3: Work a sc stitch in the next chain stitch. Work your crochet stitches into each chain across as mentioned in the pattern.

Step 4: The last stitch before turning is usually an increase stitch.

Step 5: Turn your work upside down to work into the underside of the chain stitches. You'll notice that only one loop is available, simply insert your hook in this loop. Work your stitches into each chain across.

Step 6: When finished, your last stitch should be next to the first stitch you made. You can now continue working in spirals.

Scan or visit **www.stitch. show/oval** for the video tutorial

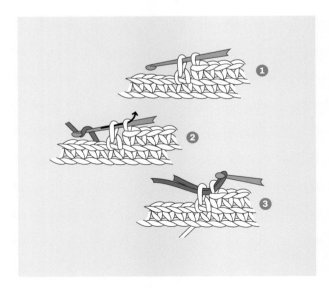

INVISIBLE COLOR CHANGE

When you want to switch from one color to the next, you work to within two stitches before a color change.

Step 1: Make the next single crochet stitch as usual, but don't pull the final loop through.

Step 2-3: Instead, wrap the new color of yarn around your hook and pull it through the remaining loops.

To make a neat color change, you can make the first stitch in the new color a slip stitch instead of a single crochet. Don't pull the slip stitch too tight or it will be difficult to crochet into in the next round. Tie the loose tails in a knot and leave them on the inside.

Scan or visit **www.stitch.show/ colorchange** for the video tutorial

FASTENING OFF

Step 1: When you've finished crocheting, cut the yarn a couple of inches / cm from your last stitch. Pull the yarn through the last loop until it is all the way through. You now have a finished knot.

Step 2: Thread the long tail through a tapestry needle and insert it through the back loop of the next stitch. This way the finishing knot will remain invisible in your finished piece. You can use this yarn tail to continue sewing the pieces together.

Scan or visit **www.stitch.show/ fastenoff** for the video tutorial

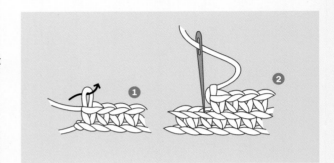

CLOSING OFF A PIECE

Step 1: After several decreases in the last round, a small hole will remain at the end of some pieces.

Step 2: Thread the yarn tail left at the end of the piece onto a yarn needle, then insert the needle through each of the front loops of the stitches in the last round. Tighten and insert the needle through the nearest stitch, make a knot, and hide the yarn tail inside the piece.

Scan or visit **www.stitch.show/ closing** for the video tutorial

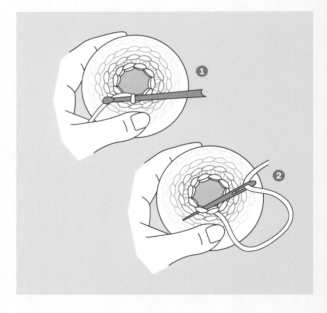

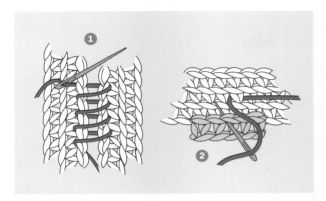

TIP: Always make sure the pieces are securely attached so that they can't be pulled off. Make small, neat stitches and try to make them show as little as possible.

TIP: Sewing pieces together with plush yarn can be challenging. If you are sewing on a larger piece, consider using **a regular acrylic or cotton yarn strand** in a coordinating color to attach the pieces. You can even split the yarn in half to work with a thinner strand for easier sewing.

JOINING PARTS — SEWING

First, pin the parts you want to sew to one another, so you can evaluate the result and adjust if necessary. If possible, use the left-over yarn tail from when you fastened off, or use a new length of the same yarn color of one of the pieces that you want to join.

Option 1 – When the different pieces are open: position the piece on the body and sew all around it, going through the stitches of both the extremity and the body.

Option 2 – When the opening of a piece is sewn closed before attaching: line up the stitches and sew through both loops of the open side and between the stitches of the closed side. Use the same color of yarn as the pieces you want to join together.

Scan or visit
**www.stitch.show/
joining-sewing**
for the video tutorial

SURFACE SINGLE CROCHET

The surface single crochet stitch is an embellishment of sc stitches worked on top of the fabric of your crochetwork.

Step 1: Use a slip knot to tie the yarn onto the crochet hook. Insert the hook around the back horizontal bar of the stitch you're working over.

Step 2: Wrap the yarn over the hook, pull that loop through.

Step 3: Wrap the yarn over the tip of the hook again and carefully pull it through both loops on the hook. This is the start of your line of surface slip stitches. Repeat this to the end of your crochetwork or in any shape you like and fasten at the back.

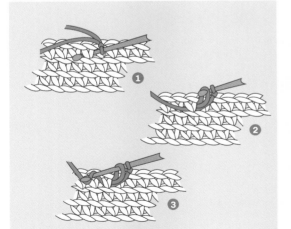

Scan or visit
**www.stitch.show/
surfacesc** for the
video tutorial

BINX
THE PLUSH BAT

Binx understands that opinions about bats can vary, but he wants to reassure everyone that he is very friendly. If you ever spot him or his friends hanging around your front porch, there's no need to worry—bats are just curious creatures with no intention of scaring anyone. Most likely, they're simply enjoying the great music you're playing or admiring your home's style.

 Solid-color bat: #6 super bulky weight yarn in • black (90 yd / 83 m) • pink (leftover for the nose) OR **Two-toned bat** • dark gray (75 yd / 69 m) • purple (15 yd / 14 m) • pink (leftover for the nose)

 H-8 / 5 mm crochet hook - Safety eyes (18 mm) - Yarn needle - Fiberfill - Pins - Optional: snaps to close the wings

 magic ring (page 17), crochet in rows (page 10)

Size: 6.5" / 16.5 cm tall when made with the indicated yarn.

 Inspiration: Scan or visit www.amigurumi.com/5201 to share your pictures or see creations made by others.

HEAD (in black yarn)

Rnd 1: start 8 sc in a magic ring [8]
Rnd 2: inc in all 8 st [16]
Rnd 3: (sc in next st, inc in next st) repeat 8 times [24]
Rnd 4: (sc in next 3 st, inc in next st) repeat 6 times [30]
Rnd 5: (sc in next 4 st, inc in next st) repeat 6 times [36]
Rnd 6 – 11: sc in all 36 st [36]
Rnd 12: (sc in next 4 st, dec) repeat 6 times [30]
Rnd 13: (sc in next 3 st, dec) repeat 6 times [24]
Rnd 14: (sc in next 2 st, dec) repeat 6 times [18]
Rnd 15: (sc in next st, dec) repeat 6 times [12]
Fasten off and weave in the yarn end. Insert the safety eyes between rounds 10-11, with 5 visible stitches in between (picture 1). Firmly press the washers onto the backs of the eyes. Stuff the head with fiberfill.

NOSE (in purple yarn)

Thread a strand of purple yarn onto your yarn needle and insert it through the opening at the bottom of the head. Sew 2 stitches between the eyes. Then weave the yarn back through to the opening at the bottom of the head and secure it with a knot to the beginning tail (pictures 2-3).

EAR (make 2, in black yarn)

Rnd 1: start 6 sc in a magic ring [6]
Rnd 2: (sc in next 2 st, inc in next st) repeat 2 times [8]
Rnd 3: (sc in next 3 st, inc in next st) repeat 2 times [10]
Rnd 4: (sc in next 4 st, inc in next st) repeat 2 times [12]
Fasten off, leaving a long tail for sewing. The ears don't need to be stuffed.
Flatten the ears and sew them to the top of the head between rounds 3 and 8, 1 round down on either side from the magic ring (picture 3).

BODY (in black yarn)

Rnd 1: start 6 sc in a magic ring [6]

Rnd 2: (sc in next st, inc in next st) repeat 3 times [9]

Rnd 3: (sc in next 2 st, inc in next st) repeat 3 times [12]

Rnd 4: (sc in next 3 st, inc in next st) repeat 3 times [15]

Rnd 5: (sc in next 4 st, inc in next st) repeat 3 times [18]

Rnd 6: (sc in next 5 st, inc in next st) repeat 3 times [21]

Rnd 7 – 10: sc in all 21 st [21]

Rnd 11: (sc in next 5 st, dec) repeat 3 times [18]

Rnd 12: (sc in next st, dec) repeat 6 times [12]

Fasten off, leaving a long tail for sewing. Stuff the body with fiberfill. Sew the 12 stitches at the top of the body to the 12 stitches at the bottom of the head (picture 4).

WING PIECE (make 2 for each wing, 4 in total, in black yarn OR make 2 in dark gray and 2 in purple yarn)

Note: There are 2 color options when making the wings,

you can make them either in a solid color (picture 7) or in 2 (contrasting) colors (picture 11). Rows 1-11 are the same for both options, but the instructions for joining the wing pieces together differ based on whether you are using a solid color or a two-tone scheme (see below).

Ch 15. Crochet in rows.

Row 1: start in second ch from the hook, sc in all 14 ch, ch 1, turn [14]

Row 2: sc in all 14 st, ch 1, turn [14]

Row 3: sc in all 14 st, do not ch 1, turn [14]

Row 4: skip 1 st, slst in next 2 st, sc in next 11 st, ch 1, turn [13]

Row 5: sc in next 11 st, ch 1, turn [11] Leave the last 2 st unworked.

Row 6: sc in all 11 st, ch 1, turn [11]

Row 7: sc in all 11 st, do not ch 1, turn [11]

Row 8: skip 1 st, slst in next 2 st, sc in next 8 st, ch 1, turn [10]

Row 9: sc in next 8 st, ch 1, turn [8] Leave the last 2 st

unworked.

Row 10: sc in next 8 st, ch 1, turn [8]

Row 11: sc in next 8 st [8]

JOINING THE SOLID-COLOR WINGS:

Fasten off on the first wing piece, leaving a long tail for sewing. Make a second wing piece, but don't fasten off. Place the wing pieces on top of each other (picture 5) and crochet the next round through both layers, along the 3 straight sides:

Closing round: sc in next 8 st, sc in next 11 st, sc in next 14 st [33]

Fasten off, leaving a long tail for sewing. Next, thread this leftover yarn tail onto your yarn needle and sew the jagged side of both wing pieces together (picture 6). Weave in all yarn tails but keep the ending yarn tail from the first wing piece, which you'll use for sewing (picture 7).

JOINING THE 2-TONE WINGS:

Fasten off on the 2 dark gray wing pieces and weave in the yarn end. Fasten off on the 2 purple wing pieces, leaving a long tail for sewing. Place the purple wing pieces on top of the dark gray pieces, with one wing facing left and the other facing right (picture 11).

The instructions differ for the left and right wing.

Left wing

Tie a new tail of dark gray yarn to your hook with a slip knot. Start crocheting in the outer corner (picture 8) and crochet the next round through both layers, along 2 straight sides (picture 8).

Closing round: sc in next 10 st up the right side, sc in next 14 st along the top side [25] (picture 9)

Fasten off, leaving a long tail for sewing. Weave the ending yarn tail through the inside of the wing and out at the inner corner, so it is in the right place to sew the wing to the body later.

Now, thread a purple yarn tail onto your yarn needle and sew all along the open straight side and the jagged side of the wing to close it, using both loops on the purple piece and only the front loops on the gray piece (picture 10). This way, your sewing stitches will not be visible from the back of the gray wing. Weave in all yarn tails, except for the long gray ending yarn tail, which you'll use for sewing (picture 11).

Right wing

Tie a new tail of dark gray yarn to your hook with a slip knot. Start crocheting in the top right corner and crochet the next round through both layers, along 2 straight sides.
Closing round: sc in next 13 st along the top side, sc in next 11 st down the side [25]
Fasten off, leaving a long tail for sewing.

Now, thread a purple yarn tail onto your yarn needle and sew all along the open straight side and the jagged side of the wing to close it, using both loops on the purple piece and only the front loops on the gray piece. This way, your sewing stitches will not be visible from the back of the gray wing.

Weave in all yarn tails, except for the long gray ending yarn tail, which you'll use for sewing.

SEWING THE WINGS TO THE BODY

Use the remaining black/dark gray yarn tail to sew the wings to the back of the body. The wings should be positioned so that they touch, but don't overlap.

Start by sewing along 5-6 stitches in the corner on the back of the wing (picture 12). Then, repeat these stitches once more to ensure the wing is securely attached.

Next, weave your yarn needle through to the front of the wing and sew 5-6 stitches along the inside of the wing to the body (picture 13). This will make the wings more sturdy (picture 14).

Note: You could sew on snaps, magnets, or velcro so you can open and close the wings. Be cautious with additional accessories when making toys for young children (picture 15).

BURKE
THE PLUSH BEE

Meet Burke, a busy little bee! When I asked him for an interview,
he buzzed, "So many flowers to visit, so little time!"
and flew off with a cheerful whir!

#6 super bulky weight yarn in
- yellow (60 yd / 55 m)
- black (25 yd / 23 m)
- white (25 yd / 23 m)
- light pink (leftover for the cheeks)

H-8 / 5 mm crochet hook -
Safety eyes (18 mm) -
Black embroidery thread
(or medium weight black yarn)
for the smile and eyebrows -
Yarn needle - Fiberfill

magic ring (page 17), crochet in
rows (page 10), changing color
(page 19)

Size: 9.5" / 24 cm tall when
made with the indicated yarn.

Inspiration: Scan or visit
www.amigurumi.com/5202 to share
your pictures or see creations
made by others.

HEAD (in yellow yarn)

Rnd 1: start 8 sc in a magic ring [8]

Rnd 2: inc in all 8 st [16]

Rnd 3: (sc in next st, inc in next st) repeat 8 times [24]

Rnd 4: (sc in next 3 st, inc in next st) repeat 6 times [30]

Rnd 5: (sc in next 4 st, inc in next st) repeat 6 times [36]

Rnd 6 – 11: sc in all 36 st [36]

Rnd 12: (sc in next 4 st, dec) repeat 6 times [30]

Rnd 13: (sc in next 3 st, dec) repeat 6 times [24]

Rnd 14: (sc in next 2 st, dec) repeat 6 times [18]

Rnd 15: (sc in next st, dec) repeat 6 times [12]

Fasten off and weave in the yarn end. Begin stuffing the head with fiberfill. Insert the safety eyes between rounds 10-11, with 5 visible stitches in between (picture 1). Firmly press the washers onto the backs of the eyes. Finish stuffing the head.

SMILE & EYEBROWS

For the smile, thread a long strand of black embroidery thread onto your yarn needle, and insert it through the opening at the bottom of the head and out between the eyes. Embroider a "V"-shape (picture 2). Weave the thread through the inside of the head and out at round 13, above the eyes. Sew a slanted stitch above each eye for the eyebrows. Weave the thread back to the inside of the head and secure it with a knot to the beginning tail (picture 3).

CHEEKS

For the cheeks, thread light pink yarn onto your yarn needle, insert it through the opening at the bottom of the head and out right below the eyes. Embroider 3 small stitches on top of each other to create each cheek (pictures 4-5). Secure your yarn with a knot and weave in the yarn ends.

ANTENNA (make 2, in black yarn)

Rnd 1: start 6 sc in a magic ring [6]

Rnd 2: inc in next st, sc in next 5 st [7]

Rnd 3: sc in all 7 st [7]

Rnd 4: dec, sc in next 3 st, dec [5]

Rnd 5 – 7: sc in all 5 st [5]

Fasten off, leaving a long tail for sewing. If you like, you can add a little bit of stuffing to the balls of the antennae. Position the antennae 1 round down on either side from the magic ring and sew them on (picture 6).

BODY (start in black yarn)

Rnd 1: start 4 sc in a magic ring [4]

Rnd 2: (sc in next st, inc in next st) repeat 2 times [6]

Rnd 3: (sc in next st, inc in next st) repeat 3 times [9]

Change to yellow yarn.

Rnd 4: slst in next st, sc in next st, inc in next st, (sc in next 2 st, inc in next st) repeat 2 times [12]

Rnd 5: (sc in next 3 st, inc in next st) repeat 3 times [15]

Rnd 6: (sc in next 4 st, inc in next st) repeat 3 times [18]

Change to black yarn.

Rnd 7: slst in next st, sc in next 4 st, inc in next st, (sc in next 5 st, inc in next st) repeat 2 times [21]

Rnd 8 – 9: sc in all 21 st [21]

Change to yellow yarn.

Rnd 10: slst in next st, sc in next 20 st [21]

Rnd 11 – 12: sc in all 21 st [21]

Change to black yarn.

Rnd 13: slst in next st, sc in next 20 st [21]

Rnd 14: (sc in next 5 st, dec) repeat 3 times [18]

Rnd 15: (sc in next 4 st, dec) repeat 3 times [15]

Change to yellow yarn.

Rnd 16: slst in next st, sc in next 2 st, dec, (sc in next 3 st, dec) repeat 2 times [12]

Fasten off, leaving a long tail for sewing. Stuff the body with fiberfill. Sew the 12 stitches at the top of the body to the 12 stitches at the bottom of the head. You may need to add a little more stuffing right before closing the seam, so that the neck joint isn't floppy (picture 7).

WING PIECE (make 2 for each wing, 4 in total, in white yarn)

Rnd 1: start 8 sc in a magic ring [8]

Rnd 2: inc in all 8 st [16]

Rnd 3: (sc in next st, inc in next st) repeat 8 times [24]

Rnd 4: (sc in next 3 st, inc in next st) repeat 6 times [30]

Rnd 5: (sc in next 4 st, inc in next st) repeat 6 times [36]

Fasten off on the first piece and weave in the yarn end (picture 8). Don't fasten off on the second wing piece. In the next round, we'll join both pieces together.

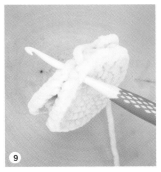

JOINING THE WING PIECES

Place the pieces on top of each other with the 'wrong' sides facing. Work the next round through both layers.

Closing round: sc in all 36 st [36] (picture 9)

Fasten off, leaving a long tail for sewing.

SEWING THE WINGS TO THE BODY

Pin the wings to the back of the body, between rounds 9-16, with 6 stitches along the edges of the wings touching each other. Sew 6-7 stitches of the wings to the body, along the front and back of the wings (picture 10). Then sew a few stitches along the join of both wings at the back, so that no stitches from the body show through (picture 11). Secure your yarn with a knot and weave in the yarn ends.

ARM (make 2, in yellow yarn)

Ch 5. Crochet in rows.

Row 1: start in second ch from the hook, sc in next 4 ch [4]

Fasten off, leaving a long tail for sewing. Sew the arms to the sides of the body, right below the head (picture 12).

BELAH
THE PLUSH BUTTERFLY

Belah can't resist a good yarn sale; she feels a special connection to yarn, though she can't quite explain why. She always buys yarn that reminds her of flowers and plans to crochet every type of flower she encounters on her daily flights.

#6 super bulky
weight yarn in
• pink (64 yd / 59 m)
• white (40 yd / 37 m)

H-8 / 5 mm crochet hook -
Safety eyes (18 mm) - Black
embroidery thread (or medium
weight black yarn) for the smile
and eyebrows - Yarn needle -
Fiberfill

magic ring (page 17), crochet in
rows (page 10), changing color
(page 19), slip stitch (page 16)

Size: 6.5" / 16.5 cm tall when
made with the indicated yarn.

Inspiration: Scan or visit
www.amigurumi.com/5203 to share your
pictures or see creations made by others.

HEAD (in pink yarn)

Rnd 1: start 8 sc in a magic ring [8]

Rnd 2: inc in all 8 st [16]

Rnd 3: (sc in next st, inc in next st) repeat 8 times [24]

Rnd 4: (sc in next 3 st, inc in next st) repeat 6 times [30]

Rnd 5: (sc in next 4 st, inc in next st) repeat 6 times [36]

Rnd 6 – 11: sc in all 36 st [36]

Rnd 12: (sc in next 4 st, dec) repeat 6 times [30]

Rnd 13: (sc in next 3 st, dec) repeat 6 times [24]

Rnd 14: (sc in next 2 st, dec) repeat 6 times [18]

Rnd 15: (sc in next st, dec) repeat 6 times [12]

Fasten off and weave in the yarn end. Insert the safety eyes between rounds 10-11, with 6-7 visible stitches in between (picture 1). Firmly press the washers onto the backs of the eyes. Stuff the head with fiberfill.

MOUTH

Thread a long piece of black embroidery thread onto your yarn needle and insert it through the opening at the bottom of the head and out between rounds 11-12. Sew 1 horizontal stitch between the eyes, then bring your needle up 1 round lower (picture 2), grab the horizontal stitch (picture 3), and insert your needle back into the same spot to create a "V" shape (picture 4). Weave the thread through the head and sew 1 small, slanted stitch over round 13 above each eye for the eyebrows (picture 4).

Weave the thread back to the inside of the head and secure it with a knot to the beginning tail.

ANTENNA (make 2, start in pink yarn)

Rnd 1: start 6 sc in a magic ring [6]

Rnd 2: inc in next st, sc in next 5 st [7]

Rnd 3: sc in all 7 st [7]

Rnd 4: dec, sc in next 3 st, dec [5]

Change to white yarn.

Rnd 5 – 7: sc in all 5 st [5]
Fasten off, leaving a long tail for sewing. If you like, you can add a little bit of stuffing to the balls of the antennae. Position the antennae 1 round down on either side from the magic ring (picture 5) and sew them on.

BODY (in pink yarn)
Rnd 1: start 4 sc in a magic ring [4]
Rnd 2: (sc in next st, inc in next st) repeat 2 times [6]
Rnd 3: (sc in next st, inc in next st) repeat 3 times [9]
Rnd 4: (sc in next 2 st, inc in next st) repeat 3 times [12]

Rnd 5: (sc in next 3 st, inc in next st) repeat 3 times [15]
Rnd 6: (sc in next 4 st, inc in next st) repeat 3 times [18]
Rnd 7: (sc in next 5 st, inc in next st) repeat 3 times [21]
Rnd 8 – 13: sc in all 21 st [21]
Rnd 14: (sc in next 5 st, dec) repeat 3 times [18]
Rnd 15: (sc in next 4 st, dec) repeat 3 times [15]
Rnd 16: (sc in next 3 st, dec) repeat 3 times [12]
Fasten off, leaving a long tail for sewing. Stuff the body with fiberfill. Sew the 12 stitches at the top of the body to the 12 stitches at the bottom of the head. You may need to add a little more stuffing right before closing the seam, so that the neck joint isn't floppy (picture 6).

WINGS

UPPER WING PIECE (make 2 for each wing, 4 in total, in white yarn)
Rnd 1: start 8 sc in a magic ring [8]
Rnd 2: inc in all 8 st [16]
Rnd 3: (sc in next st, inc in next st) repeat 8 times [24]
Rnd 4: (sc in next 3 st, inc in next st) repeat 6 times [30]
Fasten off and weave in the yarn end.

LOWER WING PIECE (make 2 for each wing, 4 in total, in white yarn)
Rnd 1: start 8 sc in a magic ring [8]

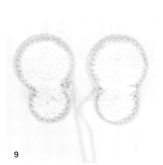
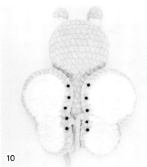

9 10 11 12

Rnd 2: inc in all 8 st [16]
Rnd 3: (sc in next 7 st, inc in next st) repeat 2 times [18]
Fasten off, leaving a long tail for sewing.
Position a lower wing piece below an upper wing piece and sew 3 stitches together to form an "8" shape (picture 7).
Repeat for all 4 wing pieces.

JOINING THE WINGS

Place 2 white wings on top of each other with the 'wrong' sides facing.
For the right wing, start crocheting on the left side in the seam between the wing pieces, and for the left wing, start crocheting on the right side in the seam (picture 8).
Tie a tail of pink yarn to your crochet hook with a slip knot and crochet all around through both sides of the wings to join them together.
Closing round: sc in all 42 st [42] (picture 9)
Just before you finish crocheting, you can tuck the pink beginning yarn tail and the white yarn tails inside the wing.
Fasten off, leaving a long tail for sewing.

Pin the wings to the back of the body with an interspace of 2 stitches (picture 10). Sew along the stitches indicated with the pins. Leave the top and bottom side of each wing unsewn (picture 11).

ARM (make 2, in pink yarn)
Ch 5. Crochet in rows.
Row 1: start in second ch from the hook, sc in next 4 ch [4]
Fasten off, leaving a long tail for sewing.
Sew the arms to the sides of the body, just below the head (picture 12).

DOTTIE
THE PLUSH DOLPHIN

Dottie has been a natural acrobat since birth. Living in the ocean makes it hard
to find balls to play with and hoops to jump through, but she's learned to be
creative with floating pieces of rubble. Every now and then, she even discovers
a bit of treasure, like a lost buoy or, once, a stray beach ball!

#6 super bulky
weight yarn in
• gray (60 yd / 55 m)
• light pink (leftover
for the cheeks)

H-8 / 5 mm crochet hook -
Safety eyes (18 mm) -
Yarn needle -
Fiberfill

magic ring (page 17)

Size: 9.5" / 25 cm long when
made with the indicated yarn.

Inspiration: Scan or visit
www.amigurumi.com/5204 to share your
pictures or see creations made by others.

HEAD & BODY (in gray yarn)

Rnd 1: start 6 sc in magic ring [6]
Rnd 2: (sc in next st, inc in next st) repeat 3 times [9]
Rnd 3 – 4: sc in all 9 st [9]
Rnd 5: (sc in next 2 st, inc in next st) repeat 3 times [12]
Rnd 6: inc in next 6 st, sc in next 6 st [18]
Rnd 7: (sc in next 2 st, inc in next st) repeat 3 times, sc in next 9 st [21]
Rnd 8: (sc in next 6 st, inc in next st) repeat 3 times [24]
Rnd 9: (sc in next 3 st, inc in next st) repeat 6 times [30]
Rnd 10: sc in all 30 st [30]
Rnd 11: (sc in next 9 st, inc in next st) repeat 3 times [33]
Rnd 12 – 16: sc in all 33 st [33]
Pause your work for a moment, do not fasten off.
Insert the safety eyes between rounds 9-10 on either side of the dolphin's head (picture 1), about 15 visible stitches apart across the top and 12 visible stitches apart across the bottom. Firmly press the washers onto the backs of the eyes.

CHEEKS

For the cheeks, thread light pink yarn onto your yarn needle. Insert it through the opening at the back of the head and out right below the eye. Embroider 2 small stitches on top of each other at the corner of each eye. Weave the yarn back through to the inside of the body and secure it with a knot to the beginning yarn end.

Continue working the body.
Rnd 17: (sc in next 9 st, dec) repeat 3 times [30]
Rnd 18: sc in all 30 st [30]
Rnd 19: (sc in next 8 st, dec) repeat 3 times [27]
Rnd 20: sc in all 27 st [27]
Stuff the body with fiberfill and continue stuffing as you go.
Rnd 21: (sc in next 7 st, dec) repeat 3 times [24]
Rnd 22: sc in all 24 st [24]
Rnd 23: (sc in next 6 st, dec) repeat 3 times [21]
Rnd 24: sc in all 21 st [21]
Rnd 25: (sc in next 5 st, dec) repeat 3 times [18]
Rnd 26: sc in all 18 st [18]
Rnd 27: (sc in next 4 st, dec) repeat 3 times [15]
Rnd 28: sc in all 15 st [15]
Rnd 29: (sc in next 3 st, dec) repeat 3 times [12]
Rnd 30: sc in all 12 st [12]
Rnd 31: (sc in next 2 st, dec) repeat 3 times [9]
Rnd 32 – 33: sc in all 9 st [9]
Rnd 34: (sc in next st, dec) repeat 3 times [6]
Fasten off, leaving a long tail for sewing.
Using a yarn needle, weave the yarn tail through the front loop of each remaining stitch (picture 2) and pull it tight to close. Weave in the yarn end (picture 3).

SIDE FIN (make 2, in gray yarn)

Rnd 1: start 4 sc in a magic ring [4]

4

5

6

Rnd 2: (sc in next st, inc in next st) repeat 2 times [6]
Rnd 3: (sc in next 2 st, inc in next st) repeat 2 times [8]
Rnd 4 − 5: sc in all 8 st [8]
Fasten off, leaving a long tail for sewing. The side fins don't need to be stuffed. Count back 3 rounds from the eyes and sew the fins to the sides of the body.

DORSAL FIN (in gray yarn)
Rnd 1: start 4 sc in a magic ring [4]
Rnd 2: inc in next st, sc in next 3 st [5]
Rnd 3: inc in next st, sc in next 4 st [6]
Rnd 4: inc in next st, sc in next 5 st [7]
Rnd 5: inc in next st, sc in next 6 st [8]
Rnd 6: inc in next st, sc in next 7 st [9]
Fasten off, leaving a long tail for sewing. The dorsal fin doesn't need to be stuffed. Sew the dorsal fin to the back, centered between the side fins, starting at round 18 of the body (or 8 rounds behind the eyes).

TAIL FIN (make 2, in gray yarn)
Rnd 1: start 4 sc in a magic ring [4]
Rnd 2: inc in next st, sc in next 3 st [5]
Rnd 3: inc in next st, sc in next 4 st [6]
Rnd 4: inc in next st, sc in next 5 st [7]
Rnd 5: inc in next st, sc in next 6 st [8]
Rnd 6: inc in next st, sc in next 7 st [9]

Rnd 7: inc in next st, sc in next 8 st [10]
Fasten off, leaving a long tail for sewing.
Align the open ends of the tail fins (picture 4) and sew them together with one of the leftover yarn tails (picture 5). Sew the joined tail fin over round 34 of the dolphin's body with the second yarn tail (picture 6).

DESSA & DUFFY
THE PLUSH DUCKS

Dessa and Duffy are a refined pair of country ducks with a passion for a good cup of tea. You might wonder how they sip tea with their beaks—it's not exactly a quiet process, but trust me, they are very polite. When they invite you over for tea, the cookies are so buttery and the tea so comforting that you won't mind the slurps and quacks along the way.

Mallard duck: #6 super bulky weight yarn in • green (50 yd / 46 m) • white (10 yd / 9 m) • tan (15 yd / 14 m) • brown (15 yd / 14 m) • yellow (10 yd / 9 m) OR **Yellow duck:** #6 super bulky weight yarn in • yellow (90 yd / 83 m) • orange (10 yd / 9 m)

Both ducks: H-8 / 5 mm crochet hook - Safety eyes (18 mm) - Black embroidery thread (or black yarn) for the eyebrows - Yarn needle - Fiberfill

Skills: magic ring (page 17), crochet in rows (page 10), changing color (page 19), slip stitch (page 16), double crochet (page 15)

Size: 6.5" / 16.5 cm tall when made with the indicated yarn.

Inspiration: Scan or visit www.amigurumi.com/5205 to share your pictures or see creations made by others.

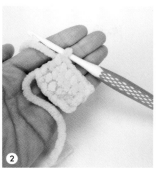
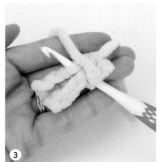

Note: In the pattern, I list the yarn colors for making a mallard duck. To make a yellow duck, make the beak and feet with orange yarn and the remaining pieces with yellow yarn. Ignore all color change instructions.

HEAD (start in green yarn)

Rnd 1: start 8 sc in a magic ring [8]

Rnd 2: inc in all 8 st [16]

Rnd 3: (sc in next st, inc in next st) repeat 8 times [24]

Rnd 4: (sc in next 7 st, inc in next st) repeat 3 times [27]

Rnd 5: (sc in next 8 st, inc in next st) repeat 3 times [30]

Rnd 6: (sc in next 9 st, inc in next st) repeat 3 times [33]

Rnd 7: sc in all 33 st [33]

Rnd 8: (sc in next 10 st, inc in next st) repeat 3 times [36]

Rnd 9: sc in all 36 st [36]

Rnd 10: (sc in next 11 st, inc in next st) repeat 3 times [39]

Rnd 11: sc in all 39 st [39]

Rnd 12: (sc in next 12 st, inc in next st) repeat 3 times [42]

Rnd 13: (sc in next 5 st, dec) repeat 6 times [36]

Rnd 14: (sc in next 4 st, dec) repeat 6 times [30]

Rnd 15: (sc in next 3 st, dec) repeat 6 times [24]

Change to white yarn.

Rnd 16: (sc in next st, dec) repeat 8 times [16]

Fasten off and weave in the yarn end. Insert the safety eyes between rounds 11-12, with 7 visible stitches in between (picture 1). Firmly press the washers onto the backs of the eyes. Stuff the head with fiberfill.

BEAK (in yellow yarn)

Ch 6. Crochet in rows.

Row 1: start in second ch from the hook, sc in next 5 ch, ch 1, turn [5]

Row 2: sc in next 5 st, ch 1, turn [5]

Row 3: sc in next 5 st [5] (picture 2)

Fold the rectangle in half, with the starting row and the ending row together. Ch 1 and work the next row through both layers to join (picture 3).

Closing row: sc in next 5 st [5]

Fasten off, leaving a long tail for sewing (picture 4).

Sew the beak to the head, between the eyes, with the sides curving down (picture 5). The corners of the beak are sewn to round 12 of the head, while the top of the beak is sewn to round 11.

For the eyebrows, thread a long piece of black embroidery thread onto your yarn needle. Insert it through the opening at the bottom of the head and back out 1 round above the eyes. Sew 1 slanted stitch above each eye, over round 14. Weave the thread back through the head to the opening and secure it with a knot to the beginning yarn end (picture 5).

BODY (start in tan yarn)
Rnd 1: start 8 sc in a magic ring [8]
Rnd 2: inc in all 8 st [16]
Rnd 3: (sc in next st, inc in next st) repeat 8 times [24]
Rnd 4: (sc in next 7 st, inc in next st) repeat 3 times [27]
Rnd 5 – 6: sc in all 27 st [27]
Change to brown yarn.
Rnd 7: sc in all 27 st [27]
Rnd 8: (sc in next 7 st, dec) repeat 3 times [24]
Rnd 9: (sc in next 6 st, dec) repeat 3 times [21]
Rnd 10: (sc in next 5 st, dec) repeat 3 times [18]
Change to white yarn.
Rnd 11: (sc in next 7 st, dec) repeat 2 times [16]
Fasten off, leaving a long tail for sewing. Stuff the body with fiberfill (picture 6). Sew the 16 stitches at the top of the body to the 16 stitches at the bottom of the head.

WING (make 2, in brown yarn)
Rnd 1: start 8 sc in a magic ring [8]
Rnd 2: inc in all 8 st [16]
Rnd 3: (sc in next st, inc in next st) repeat 8 times [24] (picture 7)
Fold the circle in half and work the next round through both layers to close the opening (picture 8)
Closing round: sc in next 12 st [12]
Fasten off, leaving a long tail for sewing (picture 9).

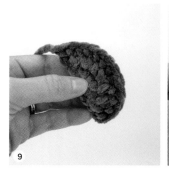

If you are making a yellow duck, sew the wings to the body right below the head.

If you are making a mallard duck, sew the wings 1 round down from where the body meets the head (so that the brown wings are sewn to the top of the brown part of the body) (picture 11).

FOOT (make 2, in yellow yarn)

Rnd 1: start 6 sc in a magic ring [6]

Rnd 2: (sc in next 2 st, inc in next st) repeat 2 times [8]

Rnd 3: (sc in next 3 st, inc in next st) repeat 2 times [10]

Rnd 4: sc in all 10 st [10]

Flatten the foot and work the next round through both layers to close the opening while making the toes.

Rnd 5: ch 1, sc + dc + sc in first st, slst in next st, sc + dc + sc in next st, slst in next st, sc + dc + sc in next st [11]

Fasten off, leaving a long tail for sewing (picture 10). Sew the feet to rounds 3-5 at the front of the body, with 1-2 stitches in between (pictures 11-12). For the mallard duck, the top of the yellow feet will be even with the brown color change line.

TAIL (in tan yarn)

Rnd 1: start 4 sc in a magic ring [4]

Rnd 2: (sc in next st, inc in next st) repeat 2 times [6]

Rnd 3: (sc in next 2 st, inc in next st) repeat 2 times [8]

Rnd 4: (sc in next 3 st, inc in next st) repeat 2 times [10]

Rnd 5: (sc in next 4 st, inc in next st) repeat 2 times [12]

Fasten off, leaving a long tail for sewing. The tail doesn't need to be stuffed. Pin and sew the tail over rounds 4-5 of the back, making sure that the duck can sit up on its own (picture 12).

DORA
THE DUMBO OCTOPUS

Dora is the happiest dumbo octopus you'll ever encounter. If you feel hesitant about calling her a dumbo octopus, don't worry—she's immensely proud of her ear-like fins. Dora dreams of meeting an elephant someday to discuss the joys of ears (or fins resembling ears) and to compare life in the deepest ocean depths with life on the African savanna.

#6 super bulky weight yarn in
• coral (50 yd / 46 m)

H-8 / 5 mm crochet hook - Safety eyes (18 mm) - Black embroidery thread (or black yarn) for the smile and eyebrows - Yarn needle - Fiberfill

magic ring (page 17), crochet in rows (page 10), slip stitch (page 16)

Size: 4" / 10 cm tall when made with the indicated yarn.

Inspiration: Scan or visit www.amigurumi.com/5206 to share your pictures or see creations made by others.

HEAD & BODY (in coral yarn)

Rnd 1: start 8 sc in a magic ring [8]
Rnd 2: inc in all 8 st [16]
Rnd 3: (sc in next st, inc in next st) repeat 8 times [24]
Rnd 4: sc in all 24 st [24]
Rnd 5: (sc in next 7 st, inc in next st) repeat 3 times [27]
Rnd 6: sc in all 27 st [27]
Rnd 7: (sc in next 8 st, inc in next st) repeat 3 times [30]
Rnd 8: sc in all 30 st [30]
Rnd 9: (sc in next 9 st, inc in next st) repeat 3 times [33]
Rnd 10: sc in all 33 st [33]
Rnd 11: (sc in next 10 st, inc in next st) repeat 3 times [36]

Fasten off and weave in the yarn end.
Insert the safety eyes between rounds 9-10, with 5 visible stitches in between. Firmly press the washers onto the backs of the eyes.

SMILE & EYEBROWS

Thread a long strand of black embroidery thread onto your yarn needle. Insert your needle through the bottom of the head and out between the eyes. Sew 1 small stitch for the smile, then weave the thread through the inside of the body and out above the eyes. Sew 1 slanted stitch above each eye for the eyebrows. Weave the thread back to the opening at the bottom of the body and secure it with a knot to the beginning tail (picture 1).

BOTTOM OF THE BODY (in coral yarn)

Rnd 1: start 8 sc in a magic ring [8]
Rnd 2: inc in all 8 st [16]
Rnd 3: (sc in next st, inc in next st) repeat 8 times [24]
Rnd 4: (sc in next 3 st, inc in next st) repeat 6 times [30]
Rnd 5: (sc in next 4 st, inc in next st) repeat 6 times [36]
Don't fasten off. In the next round, we'll join the body and the bottom piece together.

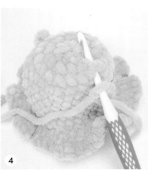

Place the bottom circle onto the body piece, with the 'right' side facing you. Insert your hook through both layers (picture 2) and work the next round through both layers to join them together. Lightly stuff the body with fiberfill at the halfway point: the octopus should hold its shape, but still be squishy.

Rnd 6: sc in all 36 st [36]
Rnd 7: inc in all 36 st [72]
Rnd 8: (sc in next st, inc in next st) repeat 36 times [108]
Fasten off, and weave in the yarn end (picture 3).

EAR FIN (make 2, in coral yarn)
Using the safety eyes as a guide, choose 2 stitches on round 4, on either side of the head, where you want to make the ear fins. Tie a new tail of coral yarn to your hook with a slip knot. Insert your hook into the first chosen stitch of round 4 (picture 4) and pull up a loop. Slst in this st.
Ch 2. Crochet in rows.
Row 1: start in second ch from the hook, sc in this ch, slst in next st on the head [2]
Fasten off and weave in the yarn tails.
Repeat for the second ear fin (pictures 5-6).

ELI
THE PLUSH ELEPHANT

Caring for plants can be challenging when you have such large feet, but Eli has made the effort to tend to his houseplants. He ensures they have good soil and fertilizer, and gently pours just enough water from his trunk to keep the plants quite content.

#6 super bulky
weight yarn in
• gray (145 yd / 133 m)

H-8 / 5 mm crochet hook -
Safety eyes (20 mm) -
Yarn needle - Fiberfill

magic ring (page 17)

Size: 10" / 25.5 cm tall when
made with the indicated yarn.

Inspiration: Scan or visit www.amigurumi.com/5207
to share your pictures or see creations made by others.

HEAD (in gray yarn)

Rnd 1: start 8 sc in a magic ring [8]

Rnd 2: inc in all 8 st [16]

Rnd 3: (sc in next st, inc in next st) repeat 8 times [24]

Rnd 4: (sc in next 3 st, inc in next st) repeat 6 times [30]

Rnd 5: (sc in next 4 st, inc in next st) repeat 6 times [36]

Rnd 6: (sc in next 5 st, inc in next st) repeat 6 times [42]

Rnd 7 – 11: sc in all 42 st [42]

Rnd 12: (sc in next 6 st, inc in next st) repeat 6 times [48]

Rnd 13: sc in all 48 st [48]

Rnd 14: (sc in next 6 st, dec) repeat 6 times [42]

Rnd 15: (sc in next 5 st, dec) repeat 6 times [36]

Rnd 16: (sc in next 4 st, dec) repeat 6 times [30]

Rnd 17: (sc in next 3 st, dec) repeat 6 times [24]

Rnd 18: (sc in next 2 st, dec) repeat 6 times [18]

Fasten off and weave in the yarn end. Begin stuffing the head with fiberfill. Insert the safety eyes between rounds 12-13, with 7 visible stitches in between (picture 1). Don't close the washers yet.

TRUNK (in gray yarn)

Rnd 1: start 8 sc in a magic ring [8]

Rnd 2: inc in next st, sc in next 7 st [9]

Rnd 3 – 13: sc in all 9 st [9]

Rnd 14: inc in all 9 st [18]

Fasten off, leaving a very long tail for sewing.

Lightly stuff the trunk with fiberfill. Sew the trunk between the eyes, at 1 stitch from either eye. Use the leftover yarn tail to create the trunk's curve. Bring your yarn needle out in a top stitch between rounds 8-9 of the trunk and insert it into a top stitch between rounds 4-5 (picture 2). Pull the yarn tail firmly (be careful to pull slowly, since chenille yarn breaks easily). Repeat if necessary.

Insert your yarn needle back into the trunk and embroider a small stitch over round 6, crossing the stitches you've just

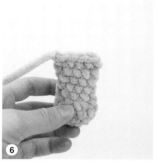

5   6   7   8

made, so that they're pulled down and blend in with your crochet fabric. Make a knot with the yarn tails and weave in the yarn ends (picture 3).

Check that the safety eyes are spaced evenly on either side of the trunk, then firmly press the washers onto the backs of the eyes. Finish stuffing the head.

EAR (make 2, in gray yarn)
Rnd 1: start 8 sc in a magic ring [8]
Rnd 2: inc in all 8 st [16]

Rnd 3: (sc in next st, inc in next st) repeat 8 times [24]
Rnd 4: (sc in next 3 st, inc in next st) repeat 6 times [30]
Rnd 5 – 7: sc in all 30 st [30]
Rnd 8: (sc in next 3 st, dec) repeat 6 times [24]
Rnd 9: (sc in next 2 st, dec) repeat 6 times [18]
Fasten off, leaving a long tail for sewing. The ears don't need to be stuffed. Flatten the ear and sew the open side to the head, about 4 stitches back from the eyes (picture 4). The tops of the ears should start at round 7. Double-check the placement of the second ear to ensure they are symmetrical.

BODY (in gray yarn)
Rnd 1: start 8 sc in a magic ring [8]
Rnd 2: inc in all 8 st [16]
Rnd 3: (sc in next st, inc in next st) repeat 8 times [24]
Rnd 4: (sc in next 3 st, inc in next st) repeat 6 times [30]
Rnd 5 – 8: sc in all 30 st [30]
Rnd 9: (sc in next 3 st, dec) repeat 6 times [24]
Rnd 10: (sc in next 2 st, dec) repeat 6 times [18]
Rnd 11 – 13: sc in all 18 st [18]
Fasten off, leaving a long tail for sewing. Stuff the body with fiberfill. Sew the 18 stitches at the top of the body to the 18 stitches at the bottom of the head.

ARM (make 2, in gray yarn)
Rnd 1: start 8 sc in a magic ring [8]

Closing round: sc in next 5 st [5]

Fasten off, leaving a long tail for sewing.

Sew the legs to the bottom of the body, covering the magic ring of the body. The legs should touch at the center of the magic ring (picture 8), so that they sit next to each other rather than sticking out to the sides.

TAIL (in gray yarn)

Rnd 1: start 5 sc in a magic ring [5]

Rnd 2 – 5: sc in all 5 st [5]

Fasten off, leaving a long tail for sewing. The tail doesn't need to be stuffed. Sew the tail to the back, between rounds 3-4 of the body.

Cut 3 short strands of #4 worsted weight yarn. Take a piece of yarn on your hook and pull it through a stitch at the tip of the tail to form a loop (picture 9), then pull the ends through this loop and make a knot. Repeat for the other strands. Trim the tail strands to about 0.75 inches / 2 cm long and pull them apart to create a fuzzy tail end (picture 10).

Rnd 2: (sc in next st, inc in next st) repeat 4 times [12]

Rnd 3 – 4: sc in all 12 st [12]

Rnd 5: (sc in next 2 st, dec) repeat 3 times [9]

Rnd 6 – 10: sc in all 9 st [9]

Stuff the arms with fiberfill. Work the next round through both layers to close the opening (picture 5). Match the stitches on both sides of the last round, leaving 1 stitch unworked at the start.

Closing round: sc in next 4 st [4]

Fasten off, leaving a long tail for sewing (picture 6). Position the arms onto the body at a slight angle, 1 round down from the head join. Sew the arms onto the body (picture 7).

LEG (make 2, in gray yarn)

Rnd 1: start 8 sc in a magic ring [8]

Rnd 2: inc in all 8 st [16]

Rnd 3: (sc in next 7 st, inc in next st) repeat 2 times [18]

Rnd 4 – 5: sc in all 18 st [18]

Rnd 6: (sc in next 4 st, dec) repeat 3 times [15]

Rnd 7: (sc in next 3 st, dec) repeat 3 times [12]

Rnd 8: (sc in next 4 st, dec) repeat 2 times [10]

Rnd 9 – 13: sc in all 10 st [10]

Stuff the legs with fiberfill. Stuff the feet firmly but leave the legs only partially stuffed. Work the next round through both layers to close the opening.

GEMMA
THE PLUSH GIRAFFE

Gemma adores making lists—daily tasks, goals, meal ideas, shopping lists, and even lists of lists she still needs to create! Some might think she's overdoing it, but Gemma thrives on organization and is undeniably the most productive giraffe you'll ever encounter.

#6 super bulky weight yarn in
• yellow (115 yd / 106 m)
• white (15 yd / 14 m)
• light brown (60 yd / 55 m)
• pink (leftover for the cheeks)

H-8 / 5 mm crochet hook -
Safety eyes (18 mm) -
Black medium weight yarn
or embroidery thread (leftover
for the eyelashes) -
Yarn needle - Fiberfill

magic ring (page 17),
changing color (page 29)

Size: 11" / 28 cm tall when
made with the indicated yarn.

Inspiration: Scan or visit
www.amigurumi.com/5208 to share your
pictures or see creations made by others.

HEAD (in yellow yarn)

Rnd 1: start 8 sc in a magic ring [8]

Rnd 2: inc in all 8 st [16]

Rnd 3: (sc in next st, inc in next st) repeat 8 times [24]

Rnd 4: (sc in next 3 st, inc in next st) repeat 6 times [30]

Rnd 5: (sc in next 4 st, inc in next st) repeat 6 times [36]

Rnd 6: (sc in next 5 st, inc in next st) repeat 6 times [42]

Rnd 7 – 11: sc in all 42 st [42]

Rnd 12: (sc in next 6 st, inc in next st) repeat 6 times [48]

Rnd 13: sc in all 48 st [48]

Rnd 14: (sc in next 6 st, dec) repeat 6 times [42]

Rnd 15: (sc in next 5 st, dec) repeat 6 times [36]

Rnd 16: (sc in next 4 st, dec) repeat 6 times [30]

Rnd 17: (sc in next 3 st, dec) repeat 6 times [24]

Rnd 18: (sc in next 2 st, dec) repeat 6 times [18]

Fasten off and weave in the yarn end. Begin stuffing the head with fiberfill. Insert the safety eyes between rounds 12-13, with 7 visible stitches in between (picture 1). Don't close the washers yet.

MUZZLE (in white yarn)

Rnd 1: start 8 sc in a magic ring [8]

Rnd 2: inc in all 8 st [16]

Rnd 3: (sc in next 7 st, inc in next st) repeat 2 times [18]

Rnd 4 – 5: sc in all 18 st [18]

Fasten off, leaving a long tail for sewing. Stuff the muzzle with fiberfill and sew it between the eyes, with the top 2 rounds above the tops of the eyes. Add more stuffing just before closing the seam.

Ensure the safety eyes are evenly spaced on either side, then firmly press the washers onto the backs of the eyes. Finish stuffing the head with fiberfill.

CHEEKS

To make the cheeks, thread pink yarn onto your yarn needle, insert it through the opening at the bottom of the head and out below the eyes. Embroider 3 small stitches on top of each other to create each cheek. Repeat for the second cheek. Weave the pink yarn back through to the opening at the bottom of the head and secure it with a knot to the beginning yarn tail (picture 2).

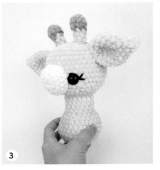

EYELASHES

To make the eyelashes, thread a long piece of medium-weight black yarn onto your yarn needle. Insert it through the opening at the bottom of the head and out just above the eyes. Embroider 1 slanted stitch above each eye and add 2 tiny eyelashes on the sides if you like. Weave the black yarn back through to the opening at the bottom of the head and secure it with a knot to the beginning tail.

BODY (in yellow yarn)

Rnd 1: start 8 sc in a magic ring [8]
Rnd 2: inc in all 8 st [16]
Rnd 3: (sc in next st, inc in next st) repeat 8 times [24]
Rnd 4: (sc in next 3 st, inc in next st) repeat 6 times [30]
Rnd 5 – 8: sc in all 30 st [30]
Rnd 9: (sc in next 3 st, dec) repeat 6 times [24]
Rnd 10: (sc in next 2 st, dec) repeat 6 times [18]
Rnd 11 – 15: sc in all 18 st [18]
Fasten off, leaving a long tail for sewing. Stuff the body with fiberfill. Sew the 18 stitches at the top of the body to the 18 stitches at the bottom of the head.

HORN (make 2, start in light brown yarn)

Rnd 1: start 6 sc in a magic ring [6]
Rnd 2: (sc in next st, inc in next st) repeat 3 times [9]
Rnd 3: sc in all 9 st [9]
Rnd 4: (sc in next st, dec) repeat 3 times [6]
Change to yellow yarn.
Rnd 5 – 7: sc in all 6 st [6]
Fasten off, leaving a long tail for sewing. Stuff only the brown tips of the horns lightly with fiberfill. Sew the horns to the top of the head, 1-2 rounds down from the magic ring.

EAR (make 2, in yellow yarn)

Rnd 1: start 4 sc in a magic ring [4]

Rnd 2: (sc in next st, inc in next st) repeat 2 times [6]

Rnd 3: (sc in next st, inc in next st) repeat 3 times [9]

Rnd 4: (sc in next 2 st, inc in next st) repeat 3 times [12]

Rnd 5: (sc in next st, inc in next st) repeat 6 times [18]

Rnd 6 − 9: sc in all 18 st [18]

Rnd 10: (sc in next st, dec) repeat 6 times [12]

Rnd 11: dec 6 times [6]

Fasten off, leaving a long tail for sewing. The ears don't need to be stuffed. Sew the ears to the head, 2-3 rounds below the horns (pictures 3-4).

ARM (make 2, start in light brown yarn)

Rnd 1: start 8 sc in a magic ring [8]

Rnd 2: (sc in next st, inc in next st) repeat 4 times [12]

Rnd 3 − 4: sc in all 12 st [12]

Rnd 5: (sc in next 2 st, dec) repeat 3 times [9]

Change to yellow yarn.

Rnd 6 − 10: sc in all 9 st [9]

Stuff the arm with fiberfill. Flatten the arm and work the next round through both layers to close the opening (picture 5). Match the stitches on both sides of the last round, leaving

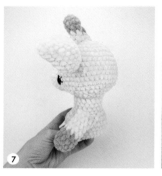

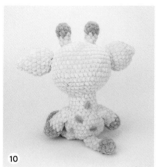

1 stitch unworked at the start.

Closing round: sc in next 4 st [4]

Fasten off, leaving a long tail for sewing (picture 6).

Pin the arms to the body, slightly angled, with the top

positioned on round 12 of the body (3 rounds down from the head) and sew them on (picture 7). Weave in the yarn ends.

LEG (make 2, start in light brown yarn)

Rnd 1: start 8 sc in a magic ring [8]

Rnd 2: inc in all 8 st [16]

Rnd 3: (sc in next 7 st, inc in next st) repeat 2 times [18]

Rnd 4 – 5: sc in all 18 st [18]

Rnd 6: (sc in next 4 st, dec) repeat 3 times [15]

Rnd 7: (sc in next 3 st, dec) repeat 3 times [12]

Change to yellow yarn.

Rnd 8: (sc in next 4 st, dec) repeat 2 times [10]

Rnd 9 – 13: sc in all 10 st [10]

Stuff the leg with fiberfill. Work the next round through both layers to close the opening.

Closing round: sc in next 5 st [5]

Fasten off, leaving a long tail for sewing.

Sew the legs to the bottom of the body. The legs should touch at the center of the magic ring (picture 8), so that they sit next to each other rather than sticking out to the sides.

TAIL (start in light brown yarn)

Rnd 1: start 8 sc in a magic ring [8]

Rnd 2: inc in next st, sc in next 7 st [9]

Rnd 3: sc in all 9 st [9]

Rnd 4: (sc in next st, dec) repeat 3 times [6]

Change to yellow yarn.

Rnd 5 – 8: sc in all 6 st [6]

Fasten off, leaving a long tail for sewing. Stuff the brown tip of the tail lightly with fiberfill. Pin the tail to rounds 3-4 at the back of the body and check to see if the giraffe can sit balanced. Sew the tail to the body.

SPOTS (in light brown yarn)

Cut a long piece of light brown yarn, knot one end and thread it onto your yarn needle. Insert your yarn needle in the giraffe's body and out where you want to embroider the first spot. Embroider a stitch that is 2-3 stitches wide (picture 9), then sew 3-4 more stitches on top to enhance visibility. Embroider as many spots as you like. The sample giraffe has 10 spots, 6 at the front and 4 at the back of the body (picture 10). You can use pins to help perfect the spot placement before embroidery.

When finished, weave the yarn back through to the starting point and secure it to the beginning tail with a knot. Weave in the yarn ends.

FLORENCE
THE PLUSH FROG

Florence, also known as Flo, adores adventure. While other frogs nap on lily pads,
Flo tests herself by attempting to hop all the way across the pond without
touching the water. Or she climbs as high as possible above the pond to
perfect her diving technique. Why does she do it? Because being a frog
is simply more exciting that way!

#6 super bulky weight yarn in
• green (75 yd / 69 m)
• light pink (leftover for
the cheeks)

H-8 / 5 mm crochet hook -
Safety eyes (18 mm) -
medium weight yarn in black
(leftover for the smile) -
Yarn needle - Fiberfill -
Optional: fabric glue

magic ring (page 17),
slip stitch (page 16)

Size: 4.5 in / 11.5 cm tall when
made with the indicated yarn.

Inspiration: Scan or visit
www.amigurumi.com/5209 to share your
pictures or see creations made by others.

HEAD & BODY (in green yarn)

Rnd 1: start 8 sc in a magic ring [8]

Rnd 2: inc in all 8 st [16]

Rnd 3: (sc in next st, inc in next st) repeat 8 times [24]

Rnd 4: (sc in next 3 st, inc in next st) repeat 6 times [30]

Rnd 5 – 7: sc in all 30 st [30]

Rnd 8: (sc in next 8 st, dec) repeat 3 times [27]

Rnd 9: sc in all 27 st [27]

Rnd 10: (sc in next 7 st, dec) repeat 3 times [24]

Rnd 11: sc in all 24 st [24]

Rnd 12: (sc in next 2 st, dec) repeat 6 times [18]

Rnd 13: sc in all 18 st [18]

Stuff the body with fiberfill and continue stuffing as you go.

Rnd 14: (sc in next st, dec) repeat 6 times [12]

Rnd 15: dec 6 times [6]

Fasten off, leaving a long tail for sewing. Using a yarn needle, weave the yarn tail through the front loop of each remaining stitch (picture 1) and pull it tight to close. Weave in the yarn end (picture 2).

EYE (make 2, in green yarn)

Rnd 1: start 6 sc in a magic ring [6]

Rnd 2: (sc in next st, inc in next st) repeat 3 times [9]

Rnd 3: sc in all 9 st [9]

Fasten off, leaving a long tail for sewing.

Insert the safety eyes between rounds 2-3 of the eyes (picture 3). Firmly press the washers onto the backs of the eyes. Sew the eyes to the top (the wider end) of the body, between rounds 2-5 (picture 4).

SMILE

For the frog's smile, cut a strand of black medium-weight yarn. Split the strand in half so you are only working with half of the original thickness of the strand. Thread the yarn onto your yarn needle, insert the needle at a random point, coming out between rounds 5 and 6. Embroider a straight stitch between rounds 5-6 (aligning with the bottom of the

eyes (picture 5)), spanning approximately 7 stitches in width. Weave the yarn back through the body to the starting point and secure it with a knot to the beginning yarn tail (picture 6). Weave in the yarn ends.

Note: To further secure the strands or any of your sewn details, pull the yarn stitch back and use a toothpick to apply a couple dots of fabric glue beneath the stitch. Then press the stitch down onto the glue.

CHEEKS

For the cheeks, thread pink yarn onto your yarn needle. Insert it into the frog's body and out right next to the smile. Embroider 2 small stitches on either side of the smile (picture 5). Weave the yarn back through the body to the starting point and secure it with a knot to the beginning yarn tail. Weave in the yarn ends.

BACK LEG (make 2, in green yarn)

Rnd 1: start 8 sc in a magic ring [8]

Rnd 2: inc in all 8 st [16]

Rnd 3: inc in next st, sc in next 15 st [17]

Rnd 4: sc in all 17 st [17]

Rnd 5: dec, sc in next 15 st [16]

Rnd 6: (sc in next 2 st, dec) repeat 4 times [12]

Rnd 7: (sc in next 4 st, dec) repeat 2 times [10]

Rnd 8: (sc in next 3 st, dec) repeat 2 times [8]

Fasten off, leaving a long tail for sewing. You can lightly stuff the back legs with fiberfill, but stuffing is optional (the back

legs in the sample are unstuffed).

BACK FOOT (make 2, in green yarn)
Rnd 1: start 8 sc in a magic ring [8]
Rnd 2 – 3: sc in all 8 st [8]
Flatten the foot and work the next round through both layers to close the opening and make the toes (picture 7).
Closing round: (sc + ch 4 + slst in next st) repeat 3 times, slst in last st [3 toes]
Fasten off, leaving a long tail for sewing.
Sew the back leg to the top of the back foot (picture 8). Then weave the leftover yarn tail from the foot to the top of the back leg for sewing the leg to the body.

FRONT LEG (make 2, in green yarn)
Rnd 1: start 4 sc in a magic ring [4]
Rnd 2: inc in next st, sc in next 3 st [5]
Rnd 3 – 4: sc in all 5 st [5]
Fasten off, leaving a long tail for sewing. The front legs don't need to be stuffed.

FRONT FOOT (make 2, in green yarn)
Rnd 1: start 6 sc in a magic ring [6]
Rnd 2 – 3: sc in all 6 st [6]
Flatten the foot and work the next round through both layers to close the opening and make the toes.
Closing round: (sc + ch 4 + slst in same st) repeat 3 times [3 toes]

Fasten off, leaving a long tail for sewing.
Sew the front leg to the top of the front foot (picture 9). Then weave the leftover yarn tail from the foot to the top of the front leg for sewing the leg to the body.

Pin the back legs to the body so that the feet are flat on the ground while the body is angled forward. The bottom of the body should be resting on the ground (pictures 10-11). Then pin the front legs to the body, at 1 stitch from the back legs, and with 5 stitches in between the top of both legs across the front. Sew the back legs to the body but leave the tops (rounds 1-3) and the feet unsewn. Sew the front legs to the body and weave in all yarn ends (picture 12).

GLORIA
THE PLUSH GOLDFISH

You might be surprised to know that many goldfish bowls actually have addresses.
After all, how else would they receive mail? For instance, Gloria resides at
106 Glass Bowlevard and eagerly welcomes any waterproof mail
you'd like to send her!

#6 super bulky
weight yarn in
• orange (50 yd / 46 m)
• pink (leftover for the
cheeks)

H-8 / 5 mm crochet hook -
black medium weight yarn or
embroidery thread (leftover
for the mouth) - Safety eyes
(18 mm) - Yarn needle - Fiberfill

magic ring (page 17),
crochet in rows (page 10)

Size: 7.5 in / 19 cm long when
made with the indicated yarn.

Inspiration: Scan or visit
www.amigurumi.com/5210 to share your
pictures or see creations made by others.

BODY (in orange yarn)

Rnd 1: start 8 sc in a magic ring [8]

Rnd 2: (sc in next st, inc in next st) repeat 4 times [12]

Rnd 3: (sc in next 3 st, inc in next st) repeat 3 times [15]

Rnd 4: (sc in next 4 st, inc in next st) repeat 3 times [18]

Rnd 5: sc in next 7 st, inc in next st, sc in next st, inc in next st (mark this inc with a stitch marker, this is the top center of the fish), sc in next st, inc in next st, sc in next 6 st [21]

Rnd 6: sc in all 21 st [21]

Rnd 7: (sc in next 6 st, inc in next st) repeat 3 times [24]

Rnd 8: (sc in next 7 st, inc in next st) repeat 3 times [27]

Rnd 9: (sc in next 8 st, inc in next st) repeat 3 times [30]

Rnd 10: sc in next 10 st, inc in next st, sc in next 13 st, inc in next st, sc in next 5 st [32]

Rnd 11: sc in all 32 st [32]

Rnd 12: (sc in next 14 st, dec) repeat 2 times [30]

Rnd 13: (sc in next 3 st, dec) repeat 6 times [24]

Pause your work and flatten the fish, with the marked stitch on round 5 at the top center. Insert the safety eyes on either side of this marked stitch, between rounds 5-6 of the body. The eyes should be about 8-9 visible stitches apart across the top and 8 stitches apart across the bottom. Firmly press the washers onto the backs of the eyes (picture 1).

MOUTH

To make the mouth, thread a piece of medium weight black yarn onto your yarn needle and insert it through the opening at the back of the body. Bring the yarn out between rounds 4-5, 2 stitches below the eyes. Embroider the mouth over 3 stitches (picture 2). Weave the yarn back through to the opening at the back of the body and secure it with a knot to the beginning tail.

CHEEKS

To make the cheeks, thread light pink yarn onto your yarn needle, insert it through the opening at the back of the body and out at the bottom corner of the eye. Sew 2 tiny stitches on top of each other to make a cheek (picture 3). Repeat for

5

6

7

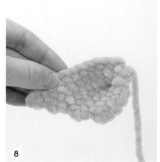
8

the second eye. Then weave the yarn back through to the opening at the back of the body and secure it with a knot to the beginning tail.

Stuff the body with fiberfill and continue stuffing as you go. Continue working the body.

Rnd 14: sc in all 24 st [24]
Rnd 15: (sc in next 2 st, dec) repeat 6 times [18]
Rnd 16: sc in all 18 st [18]
Rnd 17: (sc in next st, dec) repeat 6 times [12]
Rnd 18: sc in all 12 st [12]
Rnd 19: (sc in next 2 st, dec) repeat 3 times [9]
Fasten off, leaving a long tail for sewing. Finish stuffing the body. You want the body shape to be firm, but still narrow and "fish-like."

Using a yarn needle, weave the yarn tail through the front loop of each remaining stitch (picture 4) and pull it tight to close. Weave in the yarn end.

TAIL FIN (make 2, in orange yarn)
Ch 12. Crochet in rows.
Row 1: start in second ch from the hook, sc in next 11 ch, ch 1, turn [11]
Row 2: sc in next 10 st, do not ch 1, turn [10] Leave the last stitch unworked.
Row 3: skip 1 st, sc in next 9 st, ch 1, turn [9]
Row 4: sc in next 8 st, do not ch 1, turn [8] Leave the last stitch unworked.
Row 5: skip 1 st, sc in next 7 st, ch 1, turn [7]
Row 6: sc in next 6 st, do not ch 1, turn [6] Leave the last stitch unworked.

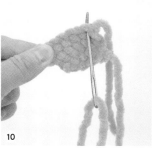

Row 7: skip 1 st, sc in next 5 st [5]

Fasten off, leaving a long yarn tail for sewing (picture 5).
Thread the yarn tail onto your yarn needle and insert it into
the bottom right corner of the tail fin, then into the center
of the right side of the fin (picture 6), then into the top
right corner (picture 7). Pull the yarn tail tight to cinch the
straight side of the fin together (picture 8) and secure it with
a knot. Leave a yarn tail for sewing.

Pin the tail fins at the back of the body, with the longer ends
at the top and bottom. Sew them in place (picture 9).

SIDE FIN (make 2, in orange yarn)

Ch 7. Crochet in rows.

Row 1: start in second ch from the hook, sc in next 6 ch,
ch 1, turn [6]

Row 2: sc in next 5 st, do not ch 1, turn [5] Leave the last
stitch unworked.

Row 3: skip 1 st, sc in next 4 st [4]

Fasten off, leaving a long tail for sewing. Thread the yarn tail
onto your yarn needle and sew the 2 corners of the straight
side of the fin together (pictures 10-11). For the right fin, you'll
need to turn the fin over and sew the corners together on the
'back' of the fin, so that both fins are mirrored. Pin the side fins
to the body, 3 rounds back from the eyes, with the longest
side facing forward. The tops of the fins should be in line with
the bottoms of the eyes (picture 12).

TOP FIN (in orange yarn)

Ch 4. Crochet in rows.

Row 1: start in second ch from the hook, sc in next 2 ch,
inc in next ch [4]

Fasten off, leaving a long tail for sewing.

Sew the top fin to the top of the body, over rounds 9-13,
2 rounds behind the safety eyes (picture 12).

JULES
THE PLUSH JELLYFISH

Never underestimate a jellyfish's ability to learn! Jules loves to read and study
and he is fascinated with what life is like above water. He is working on inventing
a special suit that will enable him to visit land and explore all the places he's read
about in books. Among 100 other places on his list, he wants to explore the
Sahara Desert, the cliffs of Ireland, and the jungles of Brazil.

#6 super bulky
weight yarn in
• light blue (60 yd / 55 m)
• dark blue (15 yd / 14 m)

H-8 / 5 mm crochet hook -
Black embroidery thread or
medium weight yarn (leftover
for the smile and eyebrows)
- Safety eyes (18 mm)
- Yarn needle - Fiberfill

magic ring (page 17),
crochet in rows (page 10)

Size: 7 in / 17.5 cm tall when
made with the indicated yarn.

Inspiration: Scan or visit
www.amigurumi.com/5211 to share your
pictures or see creations made by others.

BOTTOM CIRCLE (in blue yarn)

Rnd 1: start 8 sc in a magic ring [8]
Rnd 2: inc in all 8 st [16]
Rnd 3: (sc in next st, inc in next st) repeat 8 times [24]
Rnd 4: (sc in next 3 st, inc in next st) repeat 6 times [30]
Fasten off and weave in the yarn end.

BODY (in blue yarn)

Rnd 1: start 8 sc in a magic ring [8]
Rnd 2: inc in all 8 st [16]
Rnd 3: (sc in next st, inc in next st) repeat 8 times [24]
Rnd 4: (sc in next 7 st, inc in next st) repeat 3 times [27]
Rnd 5: (sc in next 8 st, inc in next st) repeat 3 times [30]
Rnd 6: (sc in next 9 st, inc in next st) repeat 3 times [33]
Rnd 7: sc in all 33 st [33]
Rnd 8: (sc in next 10 st, inc in next st) repeat 3 times [36]
Rnd 9: sc in all 36 st [36]
Rnd 10: (sc in next 11 st, inc in next st) repeat 3 times [39]
Rnd 11: sc in all 39 st [39]
Rnd 12: (sc in next 12 st, inc in next st) repeat 3 times [42]
Rnd 13: (sc in next 5 st, dec) repeat 6 times [36]
Rnd 14: (sc in next 4 st, dec) repeat 6 times [30]
Pause your work for a moment, do not fasten off. Insert the safety eyes between rounds 10-11 with 5-6 visible stitches in between (picture 1). Firmly press the washers onto the backs of the eyes.

MOUTH AND EYEBROWS

Thread a long strand of black embroidery thread onto your yarn needle, insert it through the opening at the bottom of the head and out between the eyes. Sew 1 horizontal stitch between the eyes, then bring your needle up 1 round lower, grab the horizontal stitch, and insert your needle back into the same spot to create a "V" shape (picture 2). Next, weave the thread through the inside of the head and out at round 8,

 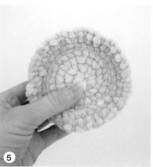  

above the eyes. Sew 1 slanted stitch above each eye for the eyebrows (picture 3). Weave the thread back through to the inside of the head and secure with a knot.

JOINING THE BODY WITH THE BOTTOM CIRCLE

Place the bottom circle onto the body piece, with the 'right' side facing you. Insert your hook through a stitch on the body and into the back loop of a stitch on the bottom circle (picture 4) and work the next round through both layers to join them together. Lightly stuff the body with fiberfill at the halfway point: the jellyfish should hold its shape, but still be squishy.

Rnd 15: slst in all 30 st [30]

Rnd 16: inc in all 30 st [60]

Note: The looser you crochet these 60 stitches, the curlier the bottom ridge will be.

Fasten off and weave in the yarn end (pictures 5-6).

CENTER TENTACLES (make 3, in dark blue yarn)

Ch 19. Crochet in rows.

Row 1: start in second ch from the hook, inc in next 18 ch [36]

Fasten off, leaving a long tail for sewing (picture 7). Sew the 3 center tentacles to the bottom of the body, covering the magic ring of the bottom circle.

OUTER TENTACLES (make 4, in blue yarn)

Ch 29. Crochet in rows.

Row 1: start in second ch from the hook, sc in next 28 ch [28]

Fasten off, leaving a long tail for sewing (picture 8). Sew the 4 tentacles around the center tentacles on the bottom circle

of the body, leaving 1-2 stitches in between each outer tentacle.

THIN TENTACLES (make 4, in dark blue yarn)
Ch 20.
Fasten off, leaving a long tail for sewing.
Since the thin tentacles are made up of only a chain, there will be a yarn tail at both ends. If you are using a plush yarn that sheds, cut the shorter, beginning yarn tail to about 2 inches / 5 cm long, then pull all the fuzz off the plush yarn strand until only the middle strings remain (picture 9). Tie these 2 strings together in a knot, at the tip of the tentacle. Cut off the excess strings, leaving only the tiny knot (picture 10). If you are using a yarn that does not shed, trim the beginning yarn tail to about 0.5 inches / 1 cm long.
Using the ending yarn tail to sew the 4 thin tentacles in between the outer tentacles on the bottom circle of the body (picture 11).

KAI
THE PLUSH KOALA

Kai's passion for cooking keeps him busy and his friends happy. You'll always find him in the kitchen——stirring, chopping, or tasting. His specialty, of course, is eucalyptus leaves, and you'd be amazed at the variety of ways he can prepare them! If you're ever in Australia, be sure to drop by and savor his latest culinary creation!

#6 super bulky weight yarn in
• gray (100 yd / 92 m)
• dark gray (10 yd / 10 m)
• white (20 yd / 19 m)

H-8 / 5 mm crochet hook -
black and white medium weight yarn
(leftover for the eye detail) - Black sewing
thread for the eyebrows - Safety eyes
(18 mm) - Yarn needle - Fiberfill

magic ring (page 17)

Size: 6 in / 15 cm tall when
made with the indicated yarn.

Inspiration: Scan or visit
www.amigurumi.com/5212 to share your
pictures or see creations made by others.

HEAD (in gray yarn)

Rnd 1: start 8 sc in a magic ring [8]

Rnd 2: inc in all 8 st [16]

Rnd 3: (sc in next st, inc in next st) repeat 8 times [24]

Rnd 4: (sc in next 3 st, inc in next st) repeat 6 times [30]

Rnd 5: (sc in next 4 st, inc in next st) repeat 6 times [36]

Rnd 6 – 9: sc in all 36 st [36]

Rnd 10: (sc in next 5 st, inc in next st) repeat 6 times [42]

Rnd 11: (sc in next 5 st, dec) repeat 6 times [36]

Rnd 12: (sc in next 4 st, dec) repeat 6 times [30]

Rnd 13: (sc in next 3 st, dec) repeat 6 times [24]

Rnd 14: (sc in next 2 st, dec) repeat 6 times [18]

Rnd 15: (sc in next 4 st, dec) repeat 3 times [15]

Fasten off and weave in the yarn end. Begin stuffing the head with fiberfill. Insert the safety eyes between rounds 10-11, with 7 visible stitches in between. Don't close the washers yet.

NOSE (in dark gray yarn)

Rnd 1: start 8 sc in a magic ring [8]

Rnd 2: (inc in next st, sc in next 3 st) repeat 2 times [10]

Slst in first st. Fasten off, leaving a long tail for sewing. Position the nose at a distance of 1 stitch between the eyes. Sew the nose to the head (picture 1). Check that the eyes are spaced evenly on either side of the nose and firmly press the washers onto the backs of the eyes.

EYELASHES

For the eyelashes, cut 1 long strand of #4 medium worsted weight yarn in black and 1 strand in white.

Thread the black strand onto your yarn needle, insert it through the opening at the bottom of the head and out above the eyes. Sew 1 slanted stitch above each eye. Weave the black yarn back through to the opening at the bottom of the head and secure with a knot.

Thread the white strand onto your yarn needle, insert it through the opening at the bottom of the head and out below the eyes. Sew 1 slanted stitch below each eye. Weave the white yarn back through to the opening at the bottom of the head and secure with a knot to the beginning end (picture 2).

EYEBROWS

For the eyebrows, cut a long strand of black embroidery thread. (Alternatively, you can use #4 medium worsted weight yarn.

Pull the strand apart into halves, so that you are only working with half of the original thickness). Take the thread onto your yarn needle, insert it through the opening at the bottom of the head, and out above the eyes. Sew 1 slanted stitch above each eye for the eyebrows. Weave the black thread back through to the opening at the bottom of the head and secure with a knot to the beginning end.

EAR (make 2, in gray yarn)

Rnd 1: start 8 sc in a magic ring [8]

Rnd 2: inc in all 8 st [16]

Rnd 3: (sc in next st, inc in next st) repeat 8 times [24]

Rnd 4 – 5: sc in all 24 st [24]

Rnd 6: (sc in next 4 st, dec) repeat 4 times [20]

The ears don't need to be stuffed.

Work the next round through both layers to close the opening (picture 3).

Closing round: sc in next 10 st [10]

Fasten off, leaving a long tail for sewing.

EAR INSERT (make 2, in white yarn)

Rnd 1: start 8 sc in a magic ring [8]

Rnd 2: inc in all 8 st [16]

Fasten off, leaving a long tail for sewing. Fit the white circle onto the front of each ear and sew in place (picture 4). Now position the ears onto the head, starting 1 round down from the beginning circle of the head (picture 5). The bottoms of the ears should be even with the bottoms of the safety eyes and 4 stitches back from the eyes (picture 6). Sew the ears to the head.

BODY (in gray yarn)

Rnd 1: start 8 sc in a magic ring [8]

Rnd 2: inc in all 8 st [16]

Rnd 3: (sc in next st, inc in next st) repeat 8 times [24]
Rnd 4: (sc in next 7 st, inc in next st) repeat 3 times [27]
Rnd 5 – 8: sc in all 27 st [27]
Rnd 9: (sc in next 7 st, dec) repeat 3 times [24]
Rnd 10: (sc in next 6 st, dec) repeat 3 times [21]
Rnd 11: (sc in next 5 st, dec) repeat 3 times [18]
Rnd 12: (sc in next 4 st, dec) repeat 3 times [15]
Fasten off, leaving a long tail for sewing. Stuff the body firmly with fiberfill. Sew the 15 stitches at the top of the body to the 15 stitches at the bottom of the head. Add more stuffing to the bottom of the head before closing the seam (picture 7).

ARM (make 2, in gray yarn)
Rnd 1: start 8 sc in a magic ring [8]
Rnd 2: inc in next st, sc in next 7 st [9]
Rnd 3: sc in all 9 st [9]
Rnd 4: dec, sc in next 5 st, dec [7]
Rnd 5 – 9: sc in all 7 st [7]
Stuff the arm with fiberfill.
Work the next round through both layers to close the opening. Match the stitches on both sides of the last round, leaving 1 stitch unworked at the start.
Closing round: sc in next 3 st [3]
Fasten off, leaving a long tail for sewing.
Position the arms horizontally onto the body, just below the head (picture 8). The arms should both face the same direction and touch so they can be sewn together. Sew the arms to the body and sew the hands together (picture 9).
Note: You could use snaps, magnets, or velcro so you can open and close the arms. Be cautious with additional accessories when making toys for young children.

LEG (make 2, in gray yarn)
Rnd 1: start 8 sc in a magic ring [8]
Rnd 2: (sc in next 3 st, inc in next st) repeat 2 times [10]
Rnd 3: sc in all 10 st [10]
Rnd 4: (sc in next 3 st, dec) repeat 2 times [8]
Rnd 5 – 9: sc in all 8 st [8]
Note: If you would like the legs to also touch each other so they can be sewn together, add 2 more rounds of 8 sc stitches after Rnd 9.
Stuff the leg with fiberfill.
Work the next round through both layers to close the opening
Closing round: sc in next 4 st [4]
Fasten off, leaving a long tail for sewing.
Position the legs horizontally onto the body, 1 round below the arms, between rounds 3 and 7 of the body (picture 10). The legs should both face the same direction. Sew the legs to the body. If you followed the original pattern, the legs will not touch at the front (picture 9). If you made the legs longer so that they can touch, you can sew the feet together.

MASON
THE PLUSH MOOSE

I would love to tell you Mason was out wandering through the woods or munching on pond lilies when I went to talk to him, but alas, it was Monday, and he was catching up on laundry. So instead, we folded towels, ironed bed sheets (he's a very genteel moose) and discussed our favorite laundry detergents.

#6 super bulky weight yarn in
- brown (90 yd / 83 m)
- dark brown (25 yd / 23 m)
- tan (15 yd / 14 m)

H-8 / 5 mm crochet hook -
Safety eyes (18 mm) -
Yarn needle - Fiberfill

magic ring (page 17),
changing colors (page 19)

Size: 7.5 in / 19 cm tall when made with the indicated yarn.

Inspiration: Scan or visit www.amigurumi.com/5213 **to share your pictures or see creations made by others.**

HEAD (in brown yarn)

Rnd 1: start 8 sc in a magic ring [8]
Rnd 2: inc in all 8 st [16]
Rnd 3: (sc in next st, inc in next st) repeat 8 times [24]
Rnd 4: (sc in next 5 st, inc in next st) repeat 4 times [28]
Rnd 5 – 9: sc in all 28 st [28]
Rnd 10: sc in next 9 st, (sc in next st, inc in next st) repeat 5 times, sc in next 9 st [33] Mark the third increase with a stitch marker for later reference.
Rnd 11: (sc in next 10 st, inc in next st) repeat 3 times [36]
Rnd 12: (sc in next 11 st, inc in next st) repeat 3 times [39]
Rnd 13: (sc in next 12 st, inc in next st) repeat 3 times [42]
Rnd 14 – 17: sc in all 42 st [42]
Rnd 18: (sc in next 5 st, dec) repeat 6 times [36]
Rnd 19: (sc in next 4 st, dec) repeat 6 times [30]
Rnd 20: (sc in next 3 st, dec) repeat 6 times [24]
The marked increase in round 10 is directed upwards. Insert the eyes between rounds 10-11 (picture 1), with 10 visible stitches between them across the top of the head. Stuff the head with fiberfill and continue stuffing as you go.
Rnd 21: (sc in next 2 st, dec) repeat 6 times [18]
Rnd 22: (sc in next st, dec) repeat 6 times [12]
Rnd 23: dec 6 times [6]
Fasten off, leaving a long tail for sewing. Using a yarn needle, weave the yarn tail through the front loop of each remaining stitch (picture 2) and pull it tight to close. Weave in the yarn end.

EAR (make 2, in brown yarn)

Rnd 1: start 4 sc in a magic ring [4]
Rnd 2: (sc in next st, inc in next st) repeat 2 times [6]
Rnd 3: (sc in next st, inc in next st) repeat 3 times [9]
Rnd 4: (sc in next 2 st, inc in next st) repeat 3 times [12]
Rnd 5: (sc in next 5 st, inc in next st) repeat 2 times [14]
Rnd 6 – 7: sc in all 14 st [14]
Rnd 8: (sc in next 5 st, dec) repeat 2 times [12]
Rnd 9: dec 6 times [6]
Fasten off, leaving a long tail for sewing. The ears don't need to be stuffed.

ANTLER (make 2, in tan yarn)

Rnd 1: start 8 sc in a magic ring [8]
Rnd 2: (sc in next 3 st, inc in next st) repeat 2 times [10]
Rnd 3: inc in first st, sc in next 9 st [11]
Rnd 4: sc in all 11 st [11]
Rnd 5: dec, sc in next 9 st [10]
Rnd 6: (sc in next 3 st, dec) repeat 2 times [8]
Rnd 7 – 11: sc in all 8 st [8]
Fasten off, leaving a long tail for sewing. Stuff the antler with fiberfill.

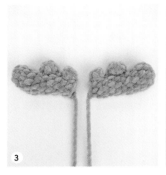

TINE #1 (make 2, in tan yarn)
Rnd 1: start 6 sc in a magic ring [6]
Rnd 2: sc in all 6 st [6]
Fasten off, leaving a long tail for sewing. Do not stuff the tine. Sew this tine to the top side of the antler, starting at the open edge of the antler.

TINE #2 (make 2, in tan yarn)
Rnd 1: start 6 sc in a magic ring [6]
Rnd 2 – 3: sc in all 6 st [6]
Fasten off, leaving a long tail for sewing. Do not stuff the tine. Sew this second tine to the top side of the antler, at 1 round from the first tine (picture 3).
Position the finished antlers and the ears onto the moose's head. Sew the ears over round 14 of the head, 3 rounds back from the safety eyes (picture 4). There are 17 stitches between the ears across the top of the head. Sew the antlers behind the ears, over rounds 15-16 of the head (picture 5). The ears should cover the bottom half of the antlers if you're looking at them from the front.

BODY (in brown yarn)
Rnd 1: start 8 sc in a magic ring [8]
Rnd 2: inc in all 8 st [16]
Rnd 3: (sc in next st, inc in next st) repeat 8 times [24]
Rnd 4: (sc in next 3 st, inc in next st) repeat 6 times [30]

Rnd 5 – 8: sc in all 30 st [30]
Rnd 9: (sc in next 8 st, dec) repeat 3 times [27]
Rnd 10: (sc in next 7 st, dec) repeat 3 times [24]
Rnd 11: (sc in next 6 st, dec) repeat 3 times [21]
Rnd 12: (sc in next 5 st, dec) repeat 3 times [18]
Rnd 13 – 14: sc in all 18 st [18]
Fasten off, leaving a long tail for sewing. Stuff the body with fiberfill. Sew the body to rounds 12-16 at the bottom of the head.

ARM (make 2, start in dark brown yarn)
Rnd 1: start 8 sc in a magic ring [8]
Rnd 2: (sc in next st, inc in next st) repeat 4 times [12]
Rnd 3 – 4: sc in all 12 st [12]

Rnd 5: (sc in next 2 st, dec) repeat 3 times [9]
Change to brown yarn.
Rnd 6 – 10: sc in all 9 st [9]
Stuff the arm with fiberfill. Stuff the hands firmly, stuff the rest of the arm only lightly.
Work the next round through both layers to close the opening (picture 6).
Closing round: sc in next 4 st [4] Leave the remaining stitch unworked.
Fasten off, leaving a long tail for sewing (picture 7).
Pin the arms onto the body, facing forward, right below the head (picture 8) and sew them on.

LEG (make 2, start in dark brown yarn)
Rnd 1: start 8 sc in a magic ring [8]
Rnd 2: inc in all 8 st [16]
Rnd 3: (sc in next 7 st, inc in next st) repeat 2 times [18]
Rnd 4 – 5: sc in all 18 st [18]
Rnd 6: (sc in next 4 st, dec) repeat 3 times [15]
Rnd 7: (sc in next 3 st, dec) repeat 3 times [12]
Change to brown yarn.
Rnd 8: (sc in next 4 st, dec) repeat 2 times [10]
Rnd 9 – 13: sc in all 10 st [10]
Stuff the leg with fiberfill. Stuff the foot firmly, stuff the rest of the leg only lightly.
Work the next round through both layers to close the opening

Closing round: sc in next 5 st [5]
Fasten off, leaving a long tail for sewing.
Sew the legs to the bottom of the body. The legs should touch at the center of the magic ring, so that they sit next to each other rather than sticking out to the sides (picture 9).

TAIL (in brown yarn)
Rnd 1: start 6 sc in a magic ring [6]
Rnd 2 – 4: sc in all 6 st [6]
Fasten off, leaving a long tail for sewing. The tail doesn't need to be stuffed. Position the tail between rounds 4-5 on your moose's back and check if your moose can sit up. Sew the tail to the body (picture 10).

MARGO
THE PLUSH MOUSE

While Margo knows it's somewhat of a stereotype for mice, she can't deny her
absolute love for snacks. Cheese is nice, but chocolate is her true favorite.
She's even contemplating opening a dessert shop tailored for tiny creatures
like herself. "It's time we rodents moved past being seen as thieves," she declared.
"No more sneaking crumbs; let's enjoy our food in a dignified manner!"

#6 super bulky
weight yarn in
• gray (75 yd / 69 m)
• light pink (20 yd / 19 m)

H-8 / 5 mm crochet hook - Black
and white medium weight yarn
(leftover for the eyelashes) -
Safety eyes (18 mm) - Yarn needle -
Fiberfill - Optional: Fabric glue

magic ring (page 17),
crochet in rows (page 10)

Size: 4 in / 10.5 cm tall when
made with the indicated yarn.

Inspiration: Scan or visit
www.amigurumi.com/5214 to share your
pictures or see creations made by others.

stitch about 10-12 times or as many times as needed to create a thick nose. Weave the yarn back through the inside of the head and secure with a knot to the beginning yarn tail.

EYELASHES

For the eyelashes, thread a strand of medium weight black yarn onto your yarn needle. Insert it through the opening at the back of the head and out above the eyes. Sew 1 stitch at an angle along the top of each eye. Weave this strand back through the inside of the head and secure with a knot. Next, thread a strand of medium worsted weight white yarn onto your yarn needle. Sew 1 white stitch below each eye. Weave this strand back through the inside of the head and secure with a knot to the beginning end (picture 2).

Note: To further secure the strands or any of your sewn details, pull the yarn stitch back and use a toothpick to apply a couple dots of fabric glue beneath the stitch. Then press the stitch down onto the glue.

Continue working the head.
Rnd 15: (sc in next 17 st, dec) repeat 2 times [36]

HEAD (in gray yarn)

Rnd 1: start 6 sc in a magic ring [6]
Rnd 2: (sc in next st, inc in next st) repeat 3 times [9]
Rnd 3: (sc in next 2 st, inc in next st) repeat 3 times [12]
Rnd 4: sc in next 4 st, inc in next st, sc in next 2 st, inc in next st, sc in next 4 st [14]
Rnd 5: sc in next 6 st, inc in next 2 st, sc in next 6 st [16]
Rnd 6: sc in next 4 st, inc in next st, (sc in next st, inc in next st) repeat 3 times, sc in next 5 st [20]
Rnd 7: (sc in next 4 st, inc in next st) repeat 4 times [24]
Rnd 8: (sc in next 3 st, inc in next st) repeat 6 times [30]
Rnd 9: (sc in next 4 st, inc in next st) repeat 6 times [36]
Rnd 10: sc in next 16 st, (sc in next st, inc in next st) repeat 2 times, sc in next 16 st [38]
Rnd 11 – 14: sc in all 38 st [38]
Pause your work for a moment, do not fasten off.
Insert the safety eyes between rounds 8-9, with about 12-13 visible stitches between the eyes, across the top of round 9. Firmly press the washers onto the backs of the eyes.

NOSE

Thread a long strand of pink yarn onto your yarn needle. Insert it through the opening at the back of the head and out through the center of the magic ring. Insert the needle back into the nose 2 rounds up (picture 1). Repeat this

Rnd 16: (sc in next 4 st, dec) repeat 6 times [30]

Rnd 17: (sc in next 3 st, dec) repeat 6 times [24]

Stuff the head with fiberfill and continue stuffing as you go.

Rnd 18: (sc in next 2 st, dec) repeat 6 times [18]

Rnd 19: (sc in next st, dec) repeat 6 times [12]

Rnd 20: dec 6 times [6]

Fasten off, leaving a long yarn tail. Using a yarn needle, weave the yarn tail through the front loop of each remaining stitch (picture 3) and pull it tight to close. Weave in the yarn end.

INNER EAR (make 2, in pink yarn)

Rnd 1: start 8 sc in a magic ring [8]

Rnd 2: inc in all 8 st [16]

Fasten off, weave in the yarn end.

EAR (make 2, in gray yarn)

Rnd 1: start 8 sc in a magic ring [8]

Rnd 2: inc in all 8 st [16]

Position a pink inner ear on top of the gray ear. Work through both loops of the outer ear and the back loops only of the inner ear (picture 4).

Joining round: sc in all 16 st [16]

Fasten off, leaving a long tail for sewing.

Weave in the beginning yarn end of the ear.

Pinch the bottom of the ear and sew 1-2 stitches together to fixate it in place (pictures 5-6).

Position and sew the ears on either side of the head, 3-4 rounds behind the eyes (picture 7).

BODY (in gray yarn)

Rnd 1: start 8 sc in a magic ring [8]

Rnd 2: inc in all 8 st [16]

Rnd 3: (sc in next st, inc in next st) repeat 8 times [24]

Rnd 4: (sc in next 3 st, inc in next st) repeat 6 times [30]

Rnd 5 – 8: sc in all 30 st [30]

Rnd 9: (sc in next 3 st, dec) repeat 6 times [24]

Rnd 10: (sc in next 2 st, dec) repeat 6 times [18]

Rnd 11: (sc in next 4 st, dec) repeat 3 times [15]

Rnd 12: sc in all 15 st [15]

Fasten off, leaving a long tail for sewing. Stuff the body with fiberfill. Sew the 15 stitches at the top of the body between rounds 11-15 of the head (picture 7).

ARM (make 2, in pink yarn)
Rnd 1: start 6 sc in a magic ring [6]
Rnd 2: (sc in next 2 st, inc in next st) repeat 2 times [8]
Rnd 3: sc in all 8 st [8]
Rnd 4: dec, sc in next 6 st [7]
Change to gray yarn.
Rnd 5 – 6: sc in all 7 st [7]
Stuff lightly with fiberfill. Work the next round through both layers to close the opening (picture 8).
Closing round: sc in next 3 st [3] Leave the remaining stitch unworked.
Fasten off, leaving a long tail for sewing (picture 9).
Position the arms onto the sides of the body, below the head, and sew them on.

FOOT (make 2, in pink yarn)
Rnd 1: start 6 sc in a magic ring [6]
Rnd 2: (sc in next 2 st, inc in next st) repeat 2 times [8]
Rnd 3: sc in all 8 st [8]
Rnd 4: dec, sc in next 6 st [7]
The foot doesn't need to be stuffed.
Work the next round through both layers to close the opening.

Closing round: sc in next 3 st [3] Leave the remaining stitch unworked.
Fasten off, leaving a long tail for sewing.
Sew the feet to rounds 2-5 on the bottom of the body, to either side of the magic ring of the body (picture 10).

TAIL (in pink yarn)
Ch 17. Crochet in rows.
Row 1: start in second ch from the hook, sc in next 16 ch [16]
Fasten off, leaving a long tail for sewing.
Position the tail between rounds 2-3 of the body and sew it on (picture 10). The tail placement will enable the mouse to stand on its own.

OSLO
THE PLUSH OWL

One year ago, Oslo's grandma taught him how to crochet, and since then, he has crafted 42 amigurumi toys. His friends are thrilled, and custom requests are flooding in. From bears and bunnies to movie characters, Oslo has done it all, but his favorite creations are birds. According to Oslo, "Crocheting arms and legs can be so tricky! Wings are definitely more enjoyable to make."

 #6 super bulky weight yarn in
- blue (60 yd / 55 m)
- yellow (10 yd / 10 m)
- cream (10 yd / 10 m)
- tan (10 yd / 10 m)

 H-8 / 5 mm crochet hook - Safety eyes (18 mm) - Yarn needle - Fiberfill

 magic ring (page 17), half double crochet (page 15), double crochet (page 15)

Size: 5 in / 12.5 cm tall when made with the indicated yarn.

Inspiration: Scan or visit www.amigurumi.com/5215 to share your pictures or see creations made by others.

EYE (make 2, start in cream yarn)

Rnd 1: start 8 sc in a magic ring [8]

Rnd 2: inc in all 8 st [16]

Change to tan yarn.

Rnd 3: (sc in next st, inc in next st) repeat 8 times [24]

Skip 1 st, slst in next st.

Fasten off, leaving a long tail for sewing (picture 1).

Insert the safety eyes off-center, between rounds 1-2 of the eye (picture 2). When working with plush yarn, close the washers. When working with cotton yarn, do not close the washers yet.

BODY (in blue yarn)

Rnd 1: start 8 sc in a magic ring [8]

Rnd 2: inc in all 8 st [16]

Rnd 3: (sc in next st, inc in next st) repeat 8 times [24]

Rnd 4: (sc in next 3 st, inc in next st) repeat 6 times [30]

Rnd 5: (sc in next 4 st, inc in next st) repeat 6 times [36]

Rnd 6: (sc in next 11 st, inc in next st) repeat 3 times [39]

Rnd 7 – 8: sc in all 39 st [39]

Rnd 9: inc in next st, sc in next 38 st [40]

Rnd 10 – 13: sc in all 40 st [40]

Rnd 14: dec, sc in next 38 st [39]

Rnd 15: sc in all 39 st [39]

Rnd 16: dec, sc in next 37 st [38]

Rnd 17 – 20: sc in all 38 st [38]

Do not fasten off. Flatten the body with the last stitch of round 20 on the left side.

Pin the eyes to the head, with the top positioned 1 round below the open top of the body, and 2 stitches in between the 2 crochet eyes.

When working with cotton yarn, insert the safety eyes through the body fabric. Firmly press the washers onto the backs of the eyes, on the inside of the body.

Sew the eyes to the body (picture 3).

  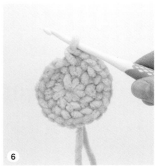 

Note: Since the top of the body is still open at this point, you can bring your needle through to the inside of the body for easy sewing. Secure your yarn with a knot on the inside of the body.

Stuff the body with fiberfill. Flatten the body with the end of round 20 on the left side, and the eyes centered. Work the next round through both layers to close the opening (picture 4).

Closing round: dc in next st, hdc in next st, sc in next 15 st, hdc in next st, dc in next st [19]

Note: Add more stuffing before closing the seam. The body should be stuffed enough to hold its shape but still be squishy.

Fasten off and weave in the yarn end (picture 5).

BEAK (in yellow yarn)
Rnd 1: start 5 sc in a magic ring [5]
Rnd 2: inc in next st, sc in next 4 st [6]
Rnd 3: sc in all 6 st [6]
Fasten off, leaving a long tail for sewing. The beak doesn't need to be stuffed. Sew the beak to the head, centered between the eyes. The bottom of the beak should be even with the bottoms of the crochet eyes.

WING (make 2, in blue yarn)
Rnd 1: start 8 sc in a magic ring [8]
Rnd 2: inc in all 8 st [16]
Rnd 3: (sc in next st, inc in next st) repeat 8 times [24] (picture 6)
Fold this circle in half.
Work the next round through both layers to close the opening (picture 7).
Closing round: sc in next 12 st [12] (picture 8)
Fasten off, leaving a long tail for sewing.
Sew the wings to the sides of the body. The rounded side is

positioned forward. The wings should be positioned diago-
nally, with the tip over round 12 of the body. Sew the back of
the wings and the top 2-3 stitches of the front of the wings,
leaving the rest of the wings unsewn (picture 9).

FOOT

Take a long strand of yellow yarn onto your yarn needle.
Insert your needle anywhere in the owl's body, leaving

several inches / cm of a beginning yarn tail, and out between
rounds 5-6 at the front. Embroider a stitch that is 2-3 stitches
wide. Sew 3 more stitches on top of this first stitch to create a
foot (pictures 10-11). Repeat for the second foot. Weave the
yarn through the inside of the owl's body and out where the
beginning yarn tail is. Tie the 2 ends in a knot and weave them
inside the owl's body.

PIPER
THE PLUSH PANDA

If you're searching for Piper, you'll always find him in his garden. While he may not have much gardening experience, his passion for plants more than compensates. When he's not watering or weeding, he's immersed in books about plants, envisioning the abundant harvest to come.

#6 super bulky weight yarn in
• white (80 yd / 74 m)
• black (80 yd / 74 m)
• pink (1 yd / 1 m)

H-8 / 5 mm crochet hook - Black medium weight yarn (for the nose and eyebrows) - Safety eyes (18 mm) - Yarn needle - Fiberfill

magic ring (page 17), crocheting around a foundation chain (page 19), surface single crochet (page 21)

Size: 10 in / 25.5 cm tall when made with the indicated yarn.

Inspiration: Scan or visit www.amigurumi.com/5216 to share your pictures or see creations made by others.

Fasten off, leaving a long tail for sewing.

Insert the safety eyes off-center between rounds 1-2 of the black spots. Place one eye toward the left side and one toward the right side (picture 1). When working with plush yarn, close the washers. When working with cotton yarn, do not close the washers yet.

Position the eye spots onto the head with the tops of the eye spots touching round 10. When working with cotton yarn, insert the safety eyes through the head fabric. Firmly press the washers onto the backs of the eyes, on the inside of the head. Sew the black spots to the head (picture 2). Stuff the head firmly with fiberfill.

HEAD (in white yarn)

Rnd 1: start 8 sc in a magic ring [8]
Rnd 2: inc in all 8 st [16]
Rnd 3: (sc in next st, inc in next st) repeat 8 times [24]
Rnd 4: (sc in next 3 st, inc in next st) repeat 6 times [30]
Rnd 5: (sc in next 4 st, inc in next st) repeat 6 times [36]
Rnd 6: (sc in next 5 st, inc in next st) repeat 6 times [42]
Rnd 7 – 11: sc in all 42 st [42]
Rnd 12: (sc in next 6 st, inc in next st) repeat 6 times [48]
Rnd 13: sc in all 48 st [48]
Rnd 14: (sc in next 6 st, dec) repeat 6 times [42]
Rnd 15: (sc in next 5 st, dec) repeat 6 times [36]
Rnd 16: (sc in next 4 st, dec) repeat 6 times [30]
Rnd 17: (sc in next 3 st, dec) repeat 6 times [24]
Rnd 18: (sc in next 2 st, dec) repeat 6 times [18]
Fasten off and weave in the yarn ends. Begin stuffing the head with fiberfill.

EYE SPOT (make 2, in black yarn)

Ch 5. Stitches are worked around both sides of the foundation chain.
Rnd 1: start in second ch from hook, sc in next 3 st, 4 sc in last st. Continue on the other side of the foundation chain, sc in next 2 st, inc in next st [11]
Rnd 2: sc in next 5 st, slst in next st [6] leave the remaining stitch unworked.

MUZZLE (in white yarn)

Rnd 1: start 8 sc in a magic ring [8]
Rnd 2: inc in all 8 st [16]
Rnd 3: (sc in next 7 st, inc in next st) repeat 2 times [18]
Rnd 4: sc in all 18 st [18]
Fasten off, leaving a long tail for sewing. Sew the muzzle between the eye spots, with the top of the muzzle at round 10, level with the tops of the black eye spots. Stuff the muzzle with fiberfill before closing the seam.

NOSE & EYEBROWS

For the nose, cut a long strand of medium weight yarn. Insert it through the opening at the bottom of the head and out between rounds 2-3 of the muzzle. Embroider 5-10 horizontal stitches for the top of the nose and 1 vertical stitch below (picture 3). Weave the black yarn through the inside of the head and out above the eyes. Sew 1 slanted stitch above each eye spot for eyebrows (picture 4). Weave the black yarn back through to the opening at the bottom of the head and secure with a knot.

CHEEKS

Thread a strand of pink yarn on your yarn needle. Insert it through the opening at the bottom of the head and out at the

bottom corner of each black eye spot. Sew 3 small stitches on top of each other to create the cheek (picture 4). Repeat for the second cheek. Weave the yarn back through to the opening at the bottom of the head and secure with a knot.

EAR (make 2, in black yarn)
Rnd 1: start 8 sc in a magic ring [8]
Rnd 2: inc in all 8 st [16]
Rnd 3 – 5: sc in all 16 st [16]
Rnd 6: (sc in next 6 st, dec) repeat 2 times [14]
Fasten off, leaving a long tail for sewing. The ears don't need to be stuffed.
Flatten the ears and sew them on both sides between rounds 4-9 of the head (picture 5).

BODY (start in white yarn)
Rnd 1: start 8 sc in a magic ring [8]
Rnd 2: inc in all 8 st [16]
Rnd 3: (sc in next st, inc in next st) repeat 8 times [24]
Rnd 4: (sc in next 3 st, inc in next st) repeat 6 times [30]
Rnd 5 – 8: sc in all 30 st [30]
Rnd 9: (sc in next 3 st, dec) repeat 6 times [24]
Change to black yarn.
Rnd 10: (sc in next 2 st, dec) repeat 6 times [18]
Rnd 11 – 12: sc in all 18 st [18]
Fasten off, leaving a long tail for sewing. Stuff the body with

fiberfill. Sew the 18 stitches at the top of the body to the 18 stitches at the bottom of the head.
Note: Because you are sewing a black piece to a white piece, if you sew on the body as usual, you will see your black stitches show through the white fabric. Therefore, insert your needle behind the post of a stitch on the head (picture 6) and behind the post of a stitch on the body (picture 7) when sewing them together (picture 8).

ARM (make 2, in black yarn)
Rnd 1: start 8 sc in a magic ring [8]
Rnd 2: (sc in next st, inc in next st) repeat 4 times [12]
Rnd 3 – 4: sc in all 12 st [12]
Rnd 5: (sc in next 2 st, dec) repeat 3 times [9]
Rnd 6 – 9: sc in all 9 st [9]
Stuff the arm with fiberfill.
Work the next round through both layers to close the opening (picture 9). Match the stitches on both sides of the last round, leaving 1 stitch unworked at the start.
Closing round: sc in next 4 st [4]
Fasten off, leaving a long tail for sewing (picture 10).
Position the arms angled onto the body, below the head, and sew them on (picture 11).

LEG (make 2, in black yarn)
Rnd 1: start 8 sc in a magic ring [8]
Rnd 2: inc in all 8 st [16]
Rnd 3: (sc in next 7 st, inc in next st) repeat 2 times [18]
Rnd 4 – 5: sc in all 18 st [18]
Rnd 6: (sc in next 4 st, dec) repeat 3 times [15]
Rnd 7: (sc in next 3 st, dec) repeat 3 times [12]
Rnd 8: (sc in next 4 st, dec) repeat 2 times [10]
Rnd 9 – 13: sc in all 10 st [10]
Stuff the leg with fiberfill. Stuff the feet tightly, stuff the leg only lightly.

Work the next round through both layers to close the opening.
Closing round: sc in next 5 st [5]
Fasten off, leaving a long tail for sewing.
Sew the legs to the bottom of the body. The legs should touch at the center of the magic ring (picture 12), so that they sit next to each other rather than sticking out to the sides.

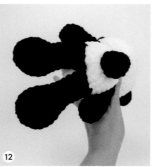

TAIL (in black yarn)
Rnd 1: start 8 sc in a magic ring [8]
Rnd 2: inc in next st, sc in next 7 st [9]
Rnd 3: sc in all 9 st [9]
Rnd 4: dec, sc in next 7 st [8]
Fasten off, leaving a long tail for sewing. The tail doesn't need to be stuffed. Sew the tail to rounds 4-5 of the body (picture 12).

BAMBOO (in green yarn)
Rnd 1: start 7 sc in a magic ring [7]
Rnd 2 – 11: sc in all 7 st [7]
Fasten off, leaving a long tail for sewing. The bamboo doesn't need to be stuffed. Using a yarn needle, weave the yarn tail through the front loop of each remaining stitch and pull it tight to close. Weave in the yarn end.

To create the ridges on the bamboo, you will be surface crocheting 3 strips around the bamboo stalk (picture 13). Tie a new tail of green yarn to your hook with a slip knot. Insert your hook 2 rounds up from the bottom of the bamboo stalk.
First ridge: surface sc in all 7 st around, slst in the first st. Fasten off and weave in the yarn ends.

Tie a new tail of green yarn to your hook with a slip knot. Insert your hook 2 rounds up from the first ridge.
Second ridge: surface sc in all 7 st around, ch 4, skip first ch on

the hook, sc in next 3 ch, slst in the first stich of the round, ch 3, skip first ch on the hook, sc in next 2 st, slst in next st on the ridge.
Fasten off and weave in the yarn ends.

Tie a new tail of green yarn to your hook with a slip knot. Insert your hook 2 rounds up from the second ridge.
Third ridge: surface sc in all 7 st around, ch 3, skip first ch on the hook, sc in next 2 ch, slst in the first stitch of the round. Fasten off and weave in the yarn ends (picture 14).

PHILO
THE PLUSH PUPPY

Philo loves nothing more than finding reasons to celebrate, give gifts, and plan surprises. For his friend Parris's birthday, he dedicated days to organizing an intricate treasure hunt at the local park. The ultimate reward waiting at the end of the hunt wasn't gold but something even better——a stash of pup treats!

#6 super bulky weight yarn in
• brown (95 yd / 87 m)
• blue (15 yd / 14 m)

H-8 / 5 mm crochet hook - Black medium weight yarn (for the snout) - Safety eyes (18 mm) - Yarn needle - Fiberfill - Optional: yarn glue

magic ring (page 17), crochet in rows (page 10)

Size: 6.5 in / 16.5 cm tall when made with the indicated yarn.

Inspiration: Scan or visit www.amigurumi.com/5217 to share your pictures or see creations made by others.

HEAD (in brown yarn)

Rnd 1: start 8 sc in a magic ring [8]
Rnd 2: inc in all 8 st [16]
Rnd 3: (sc in next st, inc in next st) repeat 8 times [24]
Rnd 4: (sc in next 3 st, inc in next st) repeat 6 times [30]
Rnd 5: (sc in next 4 st, inc in next st) repeat 6 times [36]
Rnd 6 – 9: sc in all 36 st [36]
Rnd 10: (sc in next 5 st, inc in next st) repeat 6 times [42]
Rnd 11: (sc in next 5 st, dec) repeat 6 times [36]
Rnd 12: (sc in next 4 st, dec) repeat 6 times [30]
Rnd 13: (sc in next 3 st, dec) repeat 6 times [24]
Rnd 14: (sc in next 2 st, dec) repeat 6 times [18]
Fasten off, leaving a long tail for sewing. Begin stuffing the head with fiberfill.
Insert the safety eyes between rounds 10-11 with 6 visible stitches in between (picture 1). Don't fasten the washers yet.

SNOUT (in brown yarn)

Rnd 1: start 8 sc in a magic ring [8]
Rnd 2: (sc in next st, inc in next st) repeat 4 times [12]
Rnd 3: (sc in next 5 st, inc in next st) repeat 2 times [14]
Rnd 4: sc in all 14 st [14]
Fasten off, leaving a long tail for sewing. Sew the snout between the eyes so that the top of the snout is 1 round above the tops of the eyes (picture 2). Stuff the snout with

fiberfill before closing the seam. Double check the position of the safety eyes and close the washers. Finish stuffing the head with fiberfill.

NOSE

Thread a long strand of medium weight black yarn onto your yarn needle. Insert it through the opening at the bottom of the head and out between rounds 2-3 on the snout. Sew 5-6 horizontal stitches to form the nose. Sew 1 vertical stitch below the nose (picture 2). Weave the yarn through the inside of the head to the opening at the bottom and secure with a knot.

EYE DETAIL

Thread the yarn tail leftover from the head onto your yarn needle. Weave it through the head and embroider 1 slanted stitch above and at the back of each eye (picture 3). Weave the yarn through the inside of the head to the opening at the bottom and secure with a knot.

Note: To further secure the strands or any of your sewn details, pull the yarn stitch back and use a toothpick to apply a couple dots of fabric glue beneath the stitch. Then press the stitch down onto the glue.

CHEEKS

Thread a strand of pink yarn onto your yarn needle. Insert it through the opening at the bottom of the head and out at the corner of the eye. Sew 3 tiny stitches on top of each other to form a little cheek (picture 3). Repeat on the other side. Weave the yarn through the inside of the head to the opening at the bottom and secure with a knot.

EAR (make 2, in brown yarn)

Rnd 1: start 4 sc in a magic ring [4]
Rnd 2: (sc in next st, inc in next st) repeat 2 times [6]
Rnd 3: (sc in next st, inc in next st) repeat 3 times [9]
Rnd 4: (sc in next 2 st, inc in next st) repeat 3 times [12]
Rnd 5: (sc in next 3 st, inc in next st) repeat 3 times [15]
Rnd 6: (sc in next 4 st, inc in next st) repeat 3 times [18]

Rnd 7: (sc in next 8 st, inc in next st) repeat 2 times [20]
Rnd 8 – 10: sc in all 20 st [20]
The ears don't need to be stuffed.
Work the next round through both layers to close the opening (picture 4).
Closing round: sc in next 10 st [10]
Fasten off, leaving a long tail for sewing (picture 5).
Sew the ears at an angle to the top of the head, between rounds 2-8 (pictures 6-7).

BODY (in brown yarn)
Rnd 1: start 8 sc in a magic ring [8]
Rnd 2: inc in all 8 st [16]
Rnd 3: (sc in next 7 st, inc in next st) repeat 2 times [18]
Rnd 4: (sc in next 5 st, inc in next st) repeat 3 times [21]
Rnd 5 – 8: sc in all 21 st [21]
Rnd 9: (sc in next 5 st, dec) repeat 3 times [18]
Fasten off, leaving a long tail for sewing. Stuff the body with fiberfill. Sew the 18 stitches at the top of the body to the 18 stitches at the bottom of the head (picture 7).

FRONT LEG (make 2, in brown yarn)
Rnd 1: start 8 sc in a magic ring [8]
Rnd 2 – 3: sc in all 8 st [8]
Rnd 4: (sc in next 2 st, dec) repeat 2 times [6]
Rnd 5 – 8: sc in all 6 st [6]
Stuff the feet tightly with fiberfill, stuff the legs only lightly.
Work the next round through both layers to close the opening.
Closing round: sc in next 3 st [3]
Fasten off, leaving a long tail for sewing.
Sew the front legs next to each other to the front of the puppy's body, 1 round below the head (picture 8).

BACK LEG (make 2, in brown yarn)
Rnd 1: start 8 sc in a magic ring [8]
Rnd 2: sc in all 8 st [8]

Rnd 3: (sc in next 2 st, dec) repeat 2 times [6]
Rnd 4 – 5: sc in all 6 st [6]
Stuff the legs lightly with fiberfill.
Work the next round through both layers to close the opening.
Closing round: sc in next 3 st [3]
Fasten off, leaving a long tail for sewing.
Sew the back legs to the sides of the puppy's body, over rounds 3-5 (pictures 9-10).

TAIL (in brown yarn)
Rnd 1: start 4 sc in a magic ring [4]
Rnd 2: (sc in next st, inc in next st) repeat 2 times [6]
Rnd 3: (sc in next 2 st, inc in next st) repeat 2 times [8]
Rnd 4 – 6: sc in all 8 st [8]
Rnd 7: inc in next st, sc in next 7 st [9]
Fasten off, leaving a long tail for sewing. Stuff the tail with fiberfill. Sew the tail to rounds 2-4 at the back of the body.

COLLAR (in blue yarn)
Ch 20.
Note: crochet extra chains if needed, to fit the collar around your puppy's neck.
Fasten off, leaving a long tail for sewing. Wrap the collar around the puppy's neck and tie the 2 ends in a knot. Weave the ends inside the body on the side where you will be sewing on the bow.

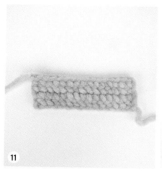

BOW (in blue yarn)

Ch 16. Crochet in rows.

Row 1: start in second ch from the hook, sc in next 15 ch, ch 1, turn [15]

Row 2 — 3: sc in next 15 st, ch 1, turn [15]

Row 4: sc in next 15 st [15]

Fasten off, leaving an extra long yarn tail (picture 11). Use this tail to sew the 2 short ends of the rectangle together forming a ring (picture 12). With the seam at the back, pinch this ring together in the middle (picture 13). Wrap the leftover yarn tail tightly around the middle—about 5-6 wraps around the bow. Use your yarn needle to pull the yarn tail through to the back of the bow and secure with a knot (picture 14). Sew the bow to the side of the collar (picture 15). Secure with a knot and weave the ends inside the body.

WILDER
THE PLUSH WHALE

The ocean seemed huge and lonely to Wilder until he met Wynn, his new friend.
Holding Wilder's fin, Wynn guided him through the ocean, showing him that other
sea creatures could become friends rather than strangers, and that the dark depths
of the ocean could be thrilling adventures rather than frightening places.

#6 super bulky
weight yarn in
• blue (90 yd / 83 m)
• white (leftover)

H-8 / 5 mm crochet hook -
White medium weight yarn (leftover
for the eye detail) - Safety eyes
(18 mm) - Yarn needle - Fiberfill -
Optional: Fabric glue

magic ring (page 17),
crochet in rows (page 10)

Size: 10 in / 25.5 cm long when
made with the indicated yarn.

Inspiration: Scan or visit
www.amigurumi.com/5218 to share your
pictures or see creations made by others.

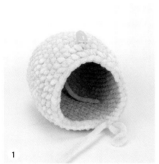

Insert the safety eyes between rounds 17-18. Using the stitch marker as your guide for the top center of the whale, place the eyes about 9 visible stitches down on either side.
Note: Ensure the eyes are evenly spaced by looking at the whale from the back (picture 2).
Firmly press the washers onto the backs of the eyes.

EYE DETAIL AND FRECKLES
Cut 2 strands of plush white yarn, and thread 1 of them onto your yarn needle. Insert it through the opening at the back of the body and out behind the eyes. Sew 3 tiny stitches behind the eye as freckles (picture 3). Weave the yarn through to the inside of the body and secure with a knot. Repeat on the other side with the second strand.
Note: Using 2 separate strands will enable you tie the knot closer to where the freckles are sewn which makes them more secure.

Take the separate piece of blue yarn and cut it into 2 strands. Thread 1 onto your yarn needle, insert it through the opening

Before you start, cut a 20" / 50 cm piece of blue yarn.

BODY (in blue yarn)
Rnd 1: start 8 sc in a magic ring [8]
Rnd 2: inc in all 8 st [16]
Rnd 3: (sc in next st, inc in next st) repeat 8 times [24]
Rnd 4: (sc in next 3 st, inc in next st) repeat 6 times [30]
Rnd 5: (sc in next 4 st, inc in next st) repeat 6 times [36]
Rnd 6: (sc in next 5 st, inc in next st) repeat 6 times [42]
Rnd 7: sc in all 42 st [42]
Rnd 8: (sc in next 13 st, inc in next st) repeat 3 times [45]
Rnd 9 – 15: sc in all 45 st [45]
Rnd 16: (sc in next 13 st, dec) repeat 3 times [42]
Rnd 17: sc in next 17 st, dec, sc in next 2 st *(mark this 2nd sc stitch with a stitch marker to indicate the top center of the whale's body (picture 1))*, dec, sc in next st, dec, sc in next 16 st [39]
Rnd 18: (sc in next 11 st, dec) repeat 3 times [36]
Rnd 19: sc in next 14 st, dec, sc in next 2 st, dec, sc in next st, dec, sc in next 13 st [33]
Rnd 20: (sc in next 9 st, dec) repeat 3 times [30]
Rnd 21: sc in next 11 st, dec, sc in next 2 st, dec, sc in next st, dec, sc in next 10 st [27]
Rnd 22: (sc in next 7 st, dec) repeat 3 times [24]
Rnd 23: (sc in next 6 st, dec) repeat 3 times [21]
Pause your work for a moment, but do not fasten off.

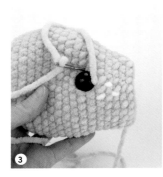

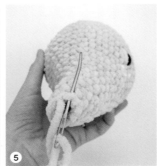

at the back of the body, and out beside the whale's eye. Sew 2 stitches above the eye (picture 3). Secure this strand with a knot and repeat with the second strand on the other side.

Lastly, cut 2 strands of medium weight white yarn. Thread 1 strand onto your yarn needle, insert it through the opening at the back of the body, and out below the whale's eye. Sew 1 stitch below the eye (picture 4). Secure this strand with a knot and repeat with the second strand on the other side. *Note: To further secure the strands or any of your sewn details, pull the yarn stitch back and use a toothpick to apply a couple dots of fabric glue beneath the stitch. Then press the stitch down onto the glue.*

Stuff the body with fiberfill and continue crocheting the body.
Rnd 24: sc in all 21 st [21]
Rnd 25: (sc in next 5 st, dec) repeat 3 times [18]
Rnd 26: sc in all 18 st [18]
Rnd 27: (sc in next 4 st, dec) repeat 3 times [15]
Rnd 28: sc in all 15 st [15]
Rnd 29: (sc in next 3 st, dec) repeat 3 times [12]
Continue stuffing the body.
Rnd 30: sc in all 12 st [12]
Rnd 31: (sc in next 2 st, dec) repeat 3 times [9]
Rnd 32: sc in all 9 st [9]

Fasten off, leaving a long tail for sewing. Using a yarn needle, weave the yarn tail through the front loop of each remaining stitch and pull it tight to close (picture 5). Weave in the yarn end (picture 6).

FLIPPERS (make 2, in blue yarn)
Rnd 1: start 4 sc in a magic ring [4]
Rnd 2: (sc in next st, inc in next st) repeat 2 times [6]
Rnd 3: (sc in next st, inc in next st) repeat 3 times [9]
Rnd 4 – 6: sc in all 9 st [9]
The flippers don't need to be stuffed.

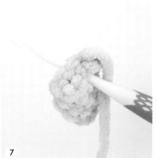

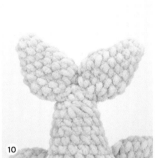

Work the next round through both layers to close the opening (picture 7).
Closing round: sc in next 4 st [4] (picture 8)
Fasten off, leaving a long tail for sewing.
Sew the flippers to the body 2 rounds behind and 2 stitches below the eyes.

TAIL FIN (make 2, in blue yarn)
Rnd 1: start 4 sc in a magic ring [4]
Rnd 2: (sc in next st, inc in next st) repeat 2 times [6]

Rnd 3: (sc in next 2 st, inc in next st) repeat 2 times [8]
Rnd 4: (sc in next 3 st, inc in next st) repeat 2 times [10]
Rnd 5: (sc in next 4 st, inc in next st) repeat 2 times [12]
Rnd 6: (sc in next 5 st, inc in next st) repeat 2 times [14]
Rnd 7: (sc in next 5 st, dec) repeat 2 times [12]
Rnd 8: (sc in next 2 st, dec) repeat 3 times [9]
Rnd 9: (sc in next st, dec) repeat 3 times [6]
Fasten off, leaving a long tail for sewing. The tail fins don't need to be stuffed. Sew the tail fins at a slight angle to the back of the body (pictures 9-10).

Theresa Kicher lives in a quiet country neighborhood in the heart of West Virginia (USA). She is delighted to share her home with her husband, two boys (ages five and seven), and a complete zoo of crocheted animals. (Don't worry, they are pretty tame as far as animals go —except for the dinosaurs who keep stirring up trouble!)

Mothering takes up the greatest part of Theresa's time these days, and she wouldn't have it any other way. She enjoys homeschooling her boys, cooking, taking trips to the library, and most of all—spending time outdoors in this beautiful world God created.

Theresa's boys help her appreciate the little things and see that you can find inspiration anywhere you look. She never lacks ideas of what to crochet next, thanks to all the animal books she reads with them, plus a constant flow of their suggestions, *"Mom, you should make a tiger shark...or a wolverine! Or a T-Rex that's taller than I am!"*

She has designed patterns for over 150 different animals, but with millions of animal species in the world, she is really just getting started!

Special thanks goes out to pattern testers Liliya Katykhin, Mai @diffuserbabies, Remy Muegge, Rosalyn @simply_rosalyn, Emily @merrybrightcrochet, @toneverlandwefly, Adrienn Weber, Amanda French, Annegret Siegert, Ashton Kirkham, Barbara Roman, Bianka Karolk-iewicz, Debbie Eastman, Dóra Sipos-Járási, Esther van Veen, Kate Waugh, Lotte Nørgaard Pedersen, Louisa Wong, Luisa Willem, Lutgarde van dijck, Marianne Rosqvist, Mariska Van den Berg, Marleen Mertens, Sandra Belleval, Sandra Zheng, Shannon Kishbaugh, Silke Bridgman, Astrid Markman, Christina Fodero , Elise Van den Poel, Ilonka Ladenius, Iris Dongo, Jasmijn van Binsbergen, Jill Constantine, Jimena Bouso, Kristi Randmaa, Serena Chew